1990

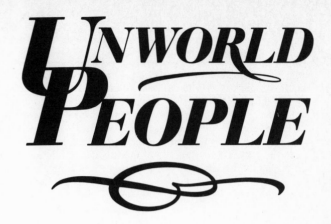

UNWORLD PEOPLE

JOYCE LANDORF HEATHERLEY

1817

HARPER & ROW, PUBLISHERS, SAN FRANCISCO

Cambridge, Hagerstown, New York, Philadelphia, Washington
London, Mexico City, São Paulo, Singapore, Sydney

Library of Congress Cataloging-in-Publication Data

Heatherley, Joyce Landorf.
  Unworld People.

    1. Consolation. 2. Christian life—1960–
3. Heatherley, Joyce Landorf. I. Title.
BV4905.2.H45 1987 248.4 87-45398
ISBN 0-06-252001-6

    88 89 90 91 HC 10 9 8 7 6 5 4 3 2

Unworld People is dedicated

To all the people who stopped running, turned, came back to me and, in God's name, helped me up so I could continue the race and hear the music once again. May you feel, dear ones, the great and glorious pleasure of God washing over your hearts and minds as we run this race together.

To the special pastor, who said, during the zenith of my unworld pain, "Joyce, you have been in the crucifixion long enough . . . now it's time to move on to the resurrection." May you know, Dr. Charles Rice, what a gift your words were to me and how God used them to bind up my brokenness.

To my husband, who never stopped believing in me and who never, even once, considered letting me give up. May you see, Francis, how clearly I have seen the face of God in the outpouring of your love . . . I will never be the same.

Joyce Landorf Heatherley

Preface

Weeping, we sat beside the rivers of Babylon thinking of Jerusalem. We have put away our lyres, hanging them upon the branches of the willow trees, for how can we sing? Yet our captors, our tormentors, demand that we sing for them the happy songs of Zion!*

I can see them. Those people there, over there, weeping and sitting beside the rivers of Babylon. Those once joyous souls, those former singers of Jerusalem, now with their throats constricting, making it impossible to sing. They've hung up their harps and lyres on the willow trees which grew by the river, bending and dipping their branches into the water's placid surface. Those people who weep, remembering their rich past, and who now recoil from their songless and unbelievable present circumstances. Those people who ask, as every generation has asked down through the centuries, "How can we sing?"

Perhaps I see those ancient, songless Hebrews more clearly and sense their suffering more intensely because of my own recent songless walk.

Several times, in the past few years, I've wanted to hang up the "will to go on." I've longed to rest. And, yes, even to weep beside some riverbank and never have to make the ef-

*Psalm 137:1–4, *The Living Bible*.

fort to sing again. More than once I've asked myself, like those ancient Israelites sitting by the rivers of Babylon, *"How can I sing?"* Or, perhaps more germane to my life, "How can I write or speak about the painful and unreal circumstances of my existence which seem to render me songless?"

Before I began this manuscript, my friend, Dr. B. D. Wells, composed these brief lines.

> Think not what might have been
> For this is now and that was then,
> Pray instead for faith to see
> What, through God's love, *today* can be.

So today, while I know it's time to write and it's time to sing . . . I will; but I do so somewhat cautiously.

It has been suggested that whenever we write of our own sufferings that, besides writing about "what might have been," we often succumb to an urge to justify our choices and actions. We authors have also been accused of sometimes using a book as a vindictive vendetta to balance out the scales a little more evenly, to right some wrongs, or to get even in some manner. The point is well taken, and realizing those potential pitfalls in writing has generated much soul searching on my part. So, carefully, I've gone over this manuscript and its message in my heart and my head, examining my soul as to my motives and my heart's intent.

While it's true that I have (for twenty-some books now) spoken and written out of past or present sufferings, I hope it can be sensed that I am not, and have not been, writing out of some need to "set the record straight."

I pray this book will bring a new perspective of hope and healing for today and for our tomorrows. For you *and* for me. I don't want to be so preoccupied with "what has been done" that I "miss what *remains* to be done."

The truth is, that after living through the most shattering

pain of my existence, both physical and emotional, I simply do not have the enormous will power or the deep reserve of strength it takes to make judgments, to take vengeance, or to assassinate another's personhood. Nor do I have the energy to say what someone else *should* have said or *should* have done.

While I know some may be afraid that this will be a bitter book, this is not true. I have experienced bitterness, anger, and even resentment, but I refuse to see my present ordeal through the dark grey lenses of those acrid, angry episodes. Neither is this writing a reporting of "scandalous" details about myself as a woman and a Christian.

At the same time, I cannot view the past unbelievable years through wholly rose-colored glasses or say that ugly rumors did not grow into greatly exaggerated, scandalous stories.

The first issue—that of writing a book laced with bitterness—would eat away like an evil-smelling acid in my soul; the second—denying these events as having taken place—would encourage me to wander about in the dense jungle of fantasy and denial. To write in either of these modes is far from the real world in which most of us live, and even farther from the reality in which I live or the personal mission statement by which I abide.

I would, then, write with a balance between transparency and honesty; and, hopefully, these pages will not be colored by grey bitterness or the rosy denial of the truth.

I must confess, though, that often in these past horrific years, I've awakened in the dead of night and wondered if the terrible pain of my body and soul would ever taper off. I'd cry, "Will I ever walk across the line or the bridge marked 'enough'? Will the rejection from others never end?" I'd ask. "Will my mind survive the torment of trudging through a crooked, winding tunnel and seeing its maddening glimpses of light which give the promise of a quick ending to my weary journey? Will I ever feel the oft remembered but seldom felt emotions of hope, peace, or joy?" I'd wonder.—

When there is a constant unreal hurricane swirling about you, giving up seems to make enormous sense. Disappearing, burrowing down a deep hole became my personal fantasy. Leaving this painful life process reinstated itself into my brain, time and time again, as the ultimate wish and dearly longed-for escape hatch.

Other people may use different routes to escape . . . drugs or alcohol, work or career, sleeping or watching TV . . . whatever! But, all escape hatches promise the same thing: relief and escape from the searing pain of our circumstances.

I wish I had some quick and simple solutions for people like us here in this "unreal" world. But alas, I've no surefire formulas (like the pamphlet I read this morning) and no glib pat-on-the-back God-bless-you's (like the well-meaning Christian lady). However, I *do* know what I *know*.

I know that often, while despairing for my life and sanity, I have crawled and sometimes dragged myself through the valley of the wounded only to find, incredibly so, that I am still alive. And, yes, while it's true that I am crushed and crumbled, bloody and battered, even bruised and beat down . . . I *am* surviving!

I know, too, the truth and reality that for all I might have wished my past relationships' circumstances to have been, the reality was that the unbelievable intensity of emotional pain, and the catastrophic leveling of my whole world, as I once knew it, has *not* annihilated me. My gifts have not vanished or even diminished, nor has my calling or my value as a person. I did not come to this truth quickly or easily, and so I still find myself surprised by this newly found self-worth.

My own recent unworld experiences have produced the most graphic and powerful lessons I could have ever learned. Not that I could have desired them or even seen them coming, for they are still almost beyond my comprehension. Exactly how learning is so enhanced and expanded by suffering, I have no idea, but I am most grateful for the wounding processes of my life and the lessons I've received from God and people during the last few years.

I found that in the process of time, and while waiting in the valley of the wounded, I had discovered something else . . . . Not the absence of pain and loneliness, no, but rather the addition of the mysterious pleasure of God's company and the surprise of His joy!

It is also awesome that I am well enough to look at Isaiah's words:

> But they that wait upon the Lord shall renew their strength. They shall mount up with wings of eagles; they shall run and not be weary; they shall walk and not faint.*

And I can accept the fact that soaring with wings of eagles and running without getting tired is simply not for me. At least not at this time. Walking, just walking and not falling down or fainting . . . ah, yes, that's about the best I can do right now. I can walk, even if it is with faltering steps, and so can you.

I can walk daring to hope again in a God who has never stopped (even for a single moment) loving and caring for me. I love the words of the great Phillips Brooks, when he wrote:

> Just as the bird is still a bird, although it cannot sing, and the rose is still a rose although its red grows dull and faded in some dark, close room where it is compelled to grow, so a Christian is still a Christian, even though his soul is dark with doubt, and he goes staggering on, fearing every moment that he will fall, never daring to look up and hope.

I am still a woman, still a Christian woman, and I can dare to

---

*Isaiah 40:31, *The Living Bible*.

look up. I can dare to hope, and so can you.

I can walk daring to wait for spring because I know I will not always be numbed by the freezing rain of rejection. For at the end of my winter's valley is the blossoming orchard of springtime's grace. I can walk feeling God's grace, and so can you.

I can walk daring to sing again because of a few rare and beautiful human beings whose compassion came from God, who cared enough to walk with me, who held me steady, and who picked me up when I fell. I can walk trusting in the care and nurturing of God and others, and so can you.

And, finally, I can walk daring to dream. I can dream about getting on with my life, about moving ahead, about finishing the race, and about being all that God intended me to be . . . including Jesus' words about the fact that He came to give us life—not mere life, but abundant life. Furthermore, I can dream not only for myself, but for all of you who are hurting. And if I can walk knowing there's meaning in my life and meaning in severe suffering, so can you.

Perhaps together, and with God's magnificent blessing and His assurance of hope, we will heal despite the brokenness of our present agony. Perhaps you and I will be able to take our first steps out of the valley of the wounded. And who knows, maybe—just maybe—when we are stronger, we will be healed enough to comfort and encourage others who are yet to experience the devastating pain and the crushing loneliness of this valley. Who knows, maybe we will even be able to sing again!

But, for now it is for you, dear suffering ones, that I write . . . from my heart.

Joyce Landorf Heatherley

Hello

Hello,
Are you broken?
I've been broken too.
I know what it's like:
    To cry in the night . . . alone,
    To scream obscenities in private rage,
    To feel the endless pit of pain,
    To soak my pillows with tears,
    To wonder when the pain will ever end,
    To wonder if I'll ever, really, be whole again,
    To ask God why I was born,
    To ask God why the pain,
    How can He use what I've got,
    How can He take a messed up life,
    And turn it into something special?
Only one who has experienced brokenness can best
Recognize
And encourage one who has been broken.
And work to encourage others who are also broken.

—Crista Hull

1

What am I doing here? . . . What makes me think I have any right to speak to these women? . . . Why did I let myself get talked into this? . . . Why didn't I just tell my friend Judy Pearson and the Chaplain that I wasn't well enough, whole enough, or healed enough to come? . . .

The sound of my own voice coming over the PA system as they play "Short Cut Home,"* from my record album, is unsettling; the sincere and caring Chaplain, the clean and simplistic beauty of the chapel—all of these things do nothing to calm my stage fright or slow down the fast, irregular pounding of my heart.

What's wrong with me? I've spoken and sung thousands of times, all over the world, for more than twenty years. This is no beginner here, no first-time-up-to-speak lady. I've been told that I am a seasoned communicator, so why do I feel so fragile inside, so ready to burst into tears, so dreadfully weary, and so out of place?

I didn't ask to come and speak before the women inmates of this Texas prison. As usual, it's always been by invitation, and I was invited. But, oh God, how can I get up from my seat and speak before these women? I'm unable to ignore the combination of the fear of failure and the high stress levels, for

*From the album, "For People Who Don't Hear the Music." Copyright © 1984. Published by Word Records.

they twist me around their little fingers, giving me a queasy stomach and a dry I-could-spit-cotton mouth. How can I move my body to the front of the chapel when I'm so paralyzed with fear?

And, if by some miracle I do make it up front, what do I say? What songs do I sing? I'm *barely* well enough to carry on a conversation or to sing one song, let alone two or three. How do I suddenly dispense wisdom for thirty or forty minutes, and how do I break forth into singing?

How dare I think that I could possibly relate to the more than two hundred women lined up in the pews around me, or they to me for that matter? These women are here for everything from felonies to heinous, violent crimes. Can we feel any personal ties between us, and is there any communion of friendship? Where is my commonality thread with their hearts and heads?

The time for me to speak comes closer and I wonder: If I am so broken, and I am; if I am so wounded, and I am; how will it be possible for me to say *anything* to the audience (or myself) which will motivate or encourage them to run the race, to persevere, and to carry on? How do I run a race when I've fallen flat on my face? And how can I get up by myself when the other runners have gone on ahead? I am alone. I lie with dirt and cinders grinding into my skin. I have been left behind and I am raw and bleeding. The women prisoners here are certainly in no shape to race, much less to hear platitudes about the joy of running or the rewards of pressing on to the finish line! How presumptuous of me to think I can communicate to them!

The Chaplain opens in prayer and then leads the spirited singing. These women love to sing. I take comfort in that, and they are very good at it. I sit there hoping they will do some extra music and, almost as though they read my mind, a group of women go to the front of the chapel and present several special numbers. Their beaming faces and our thunderous applause tells that we are all touched by their music. None more than I—because for a brief moment, while they sing, I forget I'm to be the main event.

Again, my thoughts rag at me. What if they refuse to listen? What if, when I talk, they talk, get boisterous or, heaven forbid, ignore me totally? And why shouldn't they do all of the above? Here I sit—

I, in my nice, chic little dress; they, in their white prison uniforms with only a solitary scarf and their stenciled-on names to give identity and variety to the look.

I, a newlywed clutching the hand of my beautiful "balcony person" husband, Francis. They, sitting side by side in rows, some slightly apart and as alone as space permits; some huddling in clumps, as if there is some kind of safety in numbers; still others, merging with each other as lovers do.

I, bridal radiant with love. They, lonely. I, sitting there knowing that, in an hour or two, my husband and I will be allowed to leave this prison. At the reception area, we'll sign out, a clanging iron gate will open, and then after a second gate opens, we are out. We are free. They, their minds always pondering the years, months, days, and hours left on their sentence. Others, such as our friend Judy, their minds recalling over and over how their expectations soared like helium-filled balloons only to see them pinpricked by two words: "*Parole* denied." All the inmates know they will not go home today. Someday maybe, but not today. I, grateful for escape. They, captured.

My thoughts are interrupted. The Chaplain introduces me and suddenly I am standing in front of these women looking at their expectant, upturned faces. They wait politely, attentively, as if they think I'll have something to say.

I'm sure there's never a more vulnerable feeling in the whole world than the feeling I get every time I'm in front of an audience.

I feel it now. It's more than a vague suspicion—it's a cold knowledge that, emotionally, I have no clothes on. I am naked as a blue jay, bare, au naturel, stripped. I'm convinced everyone can see my warts, moles, birthmarks, lumpiness, even my old vertical C-section scar.

If I really speak the awful, revealing truth about my life, then it won't be long before they may see something in me they don't like (and, oh dear, I do so *want* them to like me!). Or worse, they may see a weakness in me and reject me because they can't face the same weakness in themselves.

And then, what if I share the past two years of my life, and they—seeing my unhealed, still hemorrhaging scars—feel compelled to somehow try to apply emotional band-aids to my wounds? Oh, dear. Won't that make me not only visible to them, but completely vulnerable as well?

It is so risky, this business of being a leader, a teacher, a pacesetter, or whatever it is that has put me in front of others. However, now that I've been given a position of authority, I must be willing, first, to be teachable; and, secondly, to be honestly transparent. I keep hoping I'll get used to standing up and talking to people while they are all fully clothed and I feel naked.

However, this morning, there is something new happening. This morning in the prison chapel, as I struggle through this old familiar thought process, something decidedly different is taking place. Only moments before I was wondering what I'd sing or say, or how I'd communicate God's love to these women.

But now, *I see them.*
I mean, *I really see them.*

I am awestruck. What is this? A trick, an illusion, or a quirk between my brain and my eyes? Ignoring it is impossible! I see the women before me and *they all look like me. Exactly like me.*

Like me, they are naked. Like me, they have scars, warts, and lumpiness. Like me, their wounds fester and ooze. Like me, like me! They could each be my identical twin! They hurt where I hurt. They bleed where I bleed. They are broken where I am broken. And they are running or falling in the same, *the very same* race as I am.

In a few moments, the stunning effect of seeing these women, not as a collective group of prisoners but as one person just like me, begins to register in my brain. Slowly it filters down to my heart. I reason: If their *hurts* are the same as mine, then their *needs* are the same as well. Our situations and our crises may differ widely, but our brokenness is an exact match.

Prisoner or civilian, locked up or free, in our humanity we are indistinguishable from each other. Actually, I know people on the "outside" who are in just as much a prison as the inmates before me. People are people. We belong to the human race. We are one.

I want to shout, to give a joyous yell, "I know who you are! I know your name! I know it because it's my name, too!" Now I sense, with a quickening in my spirit, exactly what I'll say and sing. So I catch my breath and silently pray,

> Oh, dear God,
> Thank you for this experience.
> Thank you for these women.
> They are no different from me . . .
> I, no different from them.
>
> We have many common bonds
> Deeply interlaced and twined together.

Our thoughts, our feelings, our wounds,
Our hopes and even our dreams
Overlap because
We live in the reality of the unworld
And this unthinkable experience
Will alter our lives for all time.
We will never be the same.

Help us today to run the race together.
It's time to begin.

The Trust Of The Unexplained

Lord of my aching heart:
He was so young
*So **very** young*
With all of life before him
Exuberant, vital
Full of promise, of breathless wonder
Gifted, intelligent, sensitive
Always inquisitive
Eager to learn, to know, to do.
A dreamer, a schemer
Eyes full of merriment
Heart full of laughter
Venture in his blood
Mischief in his fingers
Challenge in his thoughts
So many plans, so many hopes
Admired by his teachers
Extolled by his friends
Loved, so dearly Lord . . .

Lord; no longer dare I beat my fists
Upon the walls of Heaven.
I am too weary, too sorrow-consumed.
I know now that ten thousand whys
Will never bring him back.
In pitch darkness I have shouted my whys.
My reward? A sea of shadowed silence.
What is left?
What more shall I ask?
Just this, dear God:

Think through me Your thoughts
Create within me Your peace
Until there is born in my aching heart
"The trust of the unexplained."

—Ruth Harms Calkin

2

This is the second time in less than a year that my husband, Francis, has been in the cardiac intensive care unit. Tests are being taken, doctors are conferring, and I've just walked the 110 steps from my husband's bed on the third floor of this sprawling hospital complex and followed the signs and arrows to the waiting room. The cold word "visitors" is missing from the door sign; in its place, I read, "Family Waiting Room." Since I'm alone and dreadfully afraid, the sign strangely warms and comforts me.

Pushing through its double doors, I'm surprised by this waiting room. Its spaciousness, the number of comfortable chairs, the expanse of windows lining these walls, the tables (one bare and another with a partially worked jigsaw puzzle), and even the boxes of extra puzzles stacked on the floor make this place quite unique.

There are eight or nine people, all strangers to me, clustered by twos and threes. I am the only one alone, yet I feel immediately accepted and they ease my tension. I feel as though I am with family. We share in some kind of camaraderie, as though we are actors in a play, bound together by the incredible traumatic drama around us. Each of us feels the oneness. Each of us knows that we have a loved one 110 steps away. I do not know any of their names, nor do they know mine, yet there seems to be recognition, respect, and a deep sensitivity to one another. The layers of denial appear to have been peeled off our souls, producing within us an unjaded awareness of the preciousness of people, of the beauty of life, and of the fragile thread between living and dying.

All of us are quiet, subdued, and wrapped in our own "waiting" thoughts, yet quick to be supportive to the others. No one deliberately intrudes on another's grieving or weeping, but all are sensitive and quickly reach out to anyone who expresses a thought, a feeling, or a fear aloud.

A doctor is perched on the arm of a chair and the family sits nervously around him. He talks openly about the patient he has just left. Gently he explains to the wife, daughter, and son-in-law, who look anxiously up at him, "We have only been able to save his life *temporarily*." Then he continues, "We may not be able to bring him back again, but we are going to do everything possible to get him through the next twenty-four hours. After that . . ." his voice trails off.

The family nod their heads, trying to understand his words and meaning. The wife, making a useless effort to dry the tears which are streaming down her face, sobs, "I can't believe this is happening!" The daughter looks toward the doctor and verbalizes what her family and others before her have thought, "It's unthinkable . . . Dad was fine yesterday! It's so unreal, so unbelievable!" The son-in-law puts a protective arm around his wife and, with his patting hand, tries to assure her of his love.

After a while, the physician leaves. The family watches him go. Then, with resignation, each member slumps down into his or her own chair and thoughts . . . each struggling to absorb medicine's strange language. Each in their own dark pocket of silence.

A woman sitting across from them, one of the other "waiting strangers," gently says to the shaken wife, "I'm so sorry about your husband." I am relieved and touched that the lady gives no solutions or advice nor does she even tell about *her* loved one who is the reason she is waiting in this place. Very simply, she just warms and comforts them with the caring blanket of her understanding.

I, too, am seated a couple of chairs from them. I've taken out my pad and clipboard. I'd like to write down my thoughts—and I do eventually—but I find I'm continually staring off the legal pad of paper into space. I keep wondering what's happening to *my* loved one in ICU, at cubical number 25, down the 110 steps.

One of the two ladies directly facing me waits until I glance across at her, and then she asks if I am cold. I'm so accustomed to being invisible and receiving rejection from almost everyone in my daily life (*shunning* is the Amish and Mennonite word for it) that I almost look around to see to whom she is talking. But, since no one is directly behind me, I smile and nod yes. Without a further word, she gets up, walks over to the thermostat, adjusts it, and comes back to her chair. Then, before she resumes her own personal vigil, she asks, "Is that better?" I answer, "Oh, yes, much better. Thank you." These days, and for the past two years, a gesture like this, or a kind word or act (even small ones) have happened so seldom that I'm at a loss for words. I find my inner soul strangely energized by the gratitude.

How paradoxical this all seems. Several months ago, I felt a connection with the 250 women prisoners to whom I spoke, and with whom I initially *thought* I had nothing in common; and now I feel cared for by these eight or nine people. How strange—for we strangers have so much in common. It's as if they are all my sisters and brothers, my real, my "now" family.

We are one, secretly bonded to each other by the glue of our unworld experience. Something unthinkable that we never dreamed of has happened to us. We are enduring, blindly going on, not sure we have the strength to wait, to fight, or even to hope and dream.

If you had asked what unworld people look like, I'd have

to tell you that, at first glance, we look pretty much like everyone else. There are no neon lights blinking over our heads, to identify whether we are in, or have been in, our unworld catastrophe. Nothing specific seems to set us apart from the rest of mankind.

We all have come from widely divergent backgrounds. We carry our share of tragic or happy memories; we recall the funny escapades of life and generally repress the painful ordeals. We have our own levels of intelligence and education; however, many of us have earned diplomas from the school of hard knocks and the soul-piercing episodes from life. We are from a milieu of unique nationalities with our own storehouses full of varied cultural treasures. We have differing physical appearances. We are of every age, encompassing the youngest child to the eldest adult. We are (financially and materially) rich, poor, or somewhere in between. We have suffered our share of the spectrum of traumatic events. We are not strangers to pain—either physical or emotional. We are not unacquainted with "grief losses." We are not unaccustomed to dealing with failures, sobering mistakes, or smashing successes. We are not novices, unaware of the pressures, stresses and conflicts of life. Nor do we consciously try to hide in denial, as some do, about those pressures in our everyday life.

In short, we are ordinary people, living out our daily routines in this world with its dichotomy of joys and sorrows, its good health and disease, its wholeness and its brokenness. Most of us have learned to accept life. We do not wish to run from life, hiding in some isolated ivory tower of denial. Nor do we raise our hearts in prayer or praise to God, in a pharisaical way, with our heads buried ostrich-like in the sand, to the searing pain or to the needs of others around us. Our heart's intent is to deal with life and people, continually responding to them in a godly way. We don't run away from God. On the contrary, we run towards Him, seeking His direction.

Unworld people are like you and me, whether they be next door neighbors, inmates in a state prison, or families waiting in a hospital. Nothing seems to set us apart from any other human beings, except—

Except—and the past years have drilled this into me—it is precisely when we think our life and journey here on earth is progressing about normal (neither terrific nor terrible) that we come up against the exact moment of our *unworld* situation. It sets up its furious clamor on our doorstep demanding its rightful due! Why others do not hear the deafening and ever-crescendoing sounds of the unworld experience, we cannot understand! We find ourselves trapped and unprepared for the devastating experience about to burst through the doorway of our souls.

Our encounter with the reality of the unworld pressures us out of the complacent womb of the ordinary and we are born into the extraordinary, undeniable *unworld* phenomenon. We become bona fide citizens of the *unworld* and our lives are forever altered.

We qualify as unworld people when the most *unthinkable,* the most *unbearable,* the most *unimaginable,* and the most *unreal* thing happens to us . . . not to someone else . . . but to us . . . to *me!*

The unworld turbulences in our lives, as I have come to recognize them, are *not* merely your usual malfunctional problems or struggles connected with being alive.

No, the unworld pandemonium of suffering is not:

- A grouping or collection of disquieting turning points.
- A normal, orderly change point.
- A predictable stress associated with transition.
- A small matter of being in physical or emotional discomfort.

- A vague sense of dissatisfaction or a simplistic case of the "blahs."
- A nagging, nuisance headache to be relieved by aspirins and a nap.
- A slight loss that is no big deal and can be easily replaced.

Absolutely Not!

We are members of the unworld when we are blown to bits and tiny pieces by the cataclysmic explosion of the *unforeseeable*, the *unscrupulous*, the *unpardonable*, the *unnegotiable*, the *unbearable*, and the *unheard of* thing. That "thing" which could never even touch us and would not dare touch us but now grabs us and rips our souls to shreds.

Perhaps you are thinking that my word *cataclysmic* is too strong a term and that I'm overreacting. Please know that I am keenly aware that the unworld experience comes to us accompanied by varying levels of agony. I would not minimize one person's shattering nor would I pronounce one unworld experience as greater than another.

Sometimes though, to the casual observer, there might be the tendency to view one person's *unworld* experience as shattering in nature and see another's experience as merely a tough break, maybe even sad, but certainly not devastating.

It is a totally different story, however, if *you* are the one feeling all the emotional effects of the unworld experience. When it's happening to you—you don't have the time or stamina to make a comparison test with others to see who has it the worst. You only know that while your circumstances, events, and participating people will differ from others', the brokenness of your heart is overwhelming, the pain you are suffering is very intense, and the war raging around you is very real.

When you come to the place where your trauma cannot be denied or ignored, it *is* cataclysmic and simply overwhelming! You understand that the unworld experience has happened to you—not to someone you've read about in the newspaper or seen on local or national TV. To you—not to someone who lives in a country halfway around the world. To you—not to a neighbor who lives down the street. To you, to your mate, to your children, to your family in your house— "Oh, dear God," you cry, "this is happening to me . . . to *me!*"

We may have felt, from time to time during our journey here on earth, that the road we traveled was a rocky, dangerous path, but at least we could see it and it *was* leading somewhere. Now suddenly, there *is* no path. It's as though we have come to the end of the trail and inches away from our feet is a sheer cliff. The path we are on drops thousands of feet below us. We never saw the precipice coming and we never dreamed the trail would end so soon or so abruptly.

Frantically, we think we'll just turn around and run back, away from the dangerous cliff; but when we do turn, we are faced with wild animals just waiting to devour us. Fear and a sense of being abandoned by everyone grips our hearts with a steel clamp. The despair is indescribable and *unprecedented* by anything we may have felt before.

Our cliff may be a ten-foot drop or it may be of sheer, solid granite that drops so far down that we have not yet hit the bottom. Despite the dizzying depth of our fall, while standing at the rugged cliff's edge, we have discovered that the phrase *"that* could never happen to me" is no longer a part of our vocabulary. We know better—it *can* happen to me and already *has!*

My unworld ordeal may, or may not be, the same as yours, because these traumatizing events come in all different shapes and sizes. But, for some of us, the unworld's pain is most piercing when:

- You are *unimaginably* shocked to discover your son or daughter's addiction to drugs or alcohol; or his or her preference for the world of homosexuals; or their pregnancy, abortion, divorce, suicide, or a most carefully-kept-secret lifestyle. You are torn apart by anguish *unequaled* by anything you have ever felt before. You cannot believe this is happening to your child. Your heartbreaking sadness seems *unlimited* and *unending.* Your feelings of failure and guilt as a parent are *unstoppable* and *uncontrollable.*

- You are a single parent, *unattached* and *unable* to share your burdens with anyone. You are weary to death of making all the decisions *alone.* You are sick of bearing the responsibility of holding down a job, rearing children, and being a homemaker, *alone.*

Even if you are fortunate enough once in awhile to find some good professional help in the area of counseling, what do you do all the rest of the time? Hear the pain and weariness in the words of this single mother with three teenagers at home, when she writes,

> I am grateful for the time my minister-counselor gives me. But what do you do with the rest of the week—when the counselor is not there—and you're falling apart at the seams? Where is the help when the kids are all screaming at one another, and *you* don't have any answers? You're tired, depressed and frustrated—and all you want to do is crawl into bed and pull up the covers until Jesus comes back.
>
> What do you do, Joyce, when you start having thoughts of crashing your car into a big tree or sinking into a comfortable, quiet, blurry psychotic coma? . . . Just escaping . . . phasing out? It sounds better to me all the time.
>
> I've been a Christian for 13-1/2 years now, and God has brought me through some of life's darkest days. But now I feel totally *unprepared* for this role of single mom of teenagers . . . it's not fair, Joyce—it's not fair!
>
> There are days when I feel I have hung on as long as I can—days when I no longer care about "Who will watch over my kids if I'm not around?" Days when the pain is so

acute—and that word *"Unfair!"* screams at me and draws me into a deep, dark, pity party. But I'm tired of smiling and pretending or wearing a false face and acting like everything is OK, "God is on the throne," and, "It'll all turn out okay—eventually." What about today? Right now?

I weep and ask God, Why me? Where is the help? Will I ever find love again? Will my fifteen-year-old son live to see his next birthday? And, can I really endure all of this?

I want to hug this single mom and tell her I agree! Her life, her circumstances, and relationships *are unreal!*

- You *undergo* the *unestimateable* physical and psychological damage of the most ultimate of all human violations . . . rape. And, as a writer for *People Magazine* recalled and recorded her thoughts about an unworld moment,

> No, this can't be true.
> No . . . No . . .
> It's a bad dream. I'll wake up soon . . .
> and . . . and . . .
> God please don't let this be real,
> No . . . Please no . . . it's not happening.
> But . . . it is.
> Someone help me.
> God, just make him stop . . .
> Please help me. Someone . . .
> I'm being raped.*

- You survive the rape only to experience another unexpected unworld blow. You find that loved ones whom you thought would understand are *unforgiving.* Your questions are *unanswered,* justice is often *unobtainable,* food becomes *uneatable,* books *unreadable,* embarrassing conversations *unavoidable.* Your testimony to authorities *uncorroborated,* your character *unrelentingly* defamed, your reputation *dis-*

---

*People Magazine, May 4, 1987.

credited and your physical and emotional health—forever *undermined*.

- You are pulverized, over the years, by a highly destructive relationship within your own family. You continually hope that the chasm between you and your "irregular person" will not remain *unbridgeable* forever. However, out of the blue comes the moment when a verbal confrontation erodes more soil away, stretching and widening the distance between you and that family member. The pain is totally *unreal*. Even as much as you would wish for death, you know you will not die from this *unbelievable* encounter. Nevertheless, now you feel that the immense chasm between you both has significantly deepened and seems forever *unbridgeable*.

- You are stunned and splintered apart by a miscarriage. No one in the family (sometimes even your husband) seems to understand your loss. No one gives you any grace to mourn—nor do they see the need for grieving! You tell no one, and stuff your sorrow deeply in your soul. Or, perhaps your baby has been born prematurely, or is gravely ill with a birth defect. The medical procedures were administered, and the doctors have now exhausted their heroic techniques. Everything seems to have been done . . . the only thing that remains is the baby's suffering. You must make a terrible choice. From somewhere deep within your viscera, an unrecognizable scream demands of the doctors in charge, "Let our precious baby go! Don't hurt my child and don't prolong the pain and suffering one moment longer!" You are torn and shredded by the *unfathomable* events.

  Then, if your baby dies, you may never know the real cause of death. Premature birth, defect, an *unfounded* genetic problem or an *undiscovered* or *unknown* disease . . . all you *do* know is that your precious baby is gone, your grief wounds are hemorrhaging and you feel *unhealable*.

  Later, you stand in the hospital *unattended* by doctors

... in the empty baby's room at home *uncomforted* by family and friends ... in the back of the church as the infants are brought forward for dedication ... and your tears are *uncontrollable.*

- You lose your job, established career, or respectable place in the professional community for *unspecified, unfair, unethical,* or *unjustified* reasons. "Foreclosure," "repossession," "Chapter Eleven," "bankruptcy," and "belly-up," which once were foreign words to you, are now tattooing themselves in clear English to the inside of your brain. The *unmistakable* fear of failure suddenly has come true and you are *unable* to face others or to pick up the *unmendable* pieces of your battered ego or shattered emotions.

- You stand by the bed of an aged mother or father and watch in stunned *unbelief* as a disease like cancer, stroke, or some variation of Alzheimer's disease depletes their body and mind. Before your eyes, the familiar face and figure of one so beloved deteriorates and becomes *unrecognizable.* In their bed, a stranger takes their place. Your hurt is so great that it blocks out most of the kind and caring efforts of others. You remain *uncomforted* in the cocoon of your pain. The outrage of your mind is *unappeased* and the grief of your soul is *unassuagable.*

- You enter the sphere of mid-life. Suddenly, with clarity and sinking heart, you see yourself in December's mirror. You see your high-priority goals and longed-for achievements of your youth as *unobtainable* now, your plans for the future *untouched,* and your past dreams *unfulfilled.* You are like former President Gerald Ford's wife, Betty, when she described her descent into the world of the chemically addicted in *People Magazine:*

> I was crushed by the [Presidential election] defeat. I had to uproot myself from the East for a new life in California. Our children were gone and my husband was busy trying

to make a life after politics. It was a tremendous letdown.

I felt very much alone, *unwanted* by my family and *unnec-essary*. The truth is that I was at the end of my rope.*

You whip yourself with the guilt of the *unfinished* tasks of your days. You want to be remembered for having made a difference in your world—but wonder if anyone will even *notice* your passing. Your situational depression, which had recurred on a once-in-a-while basis, seems to intensify to chronic daily depression, and you race to your own private escape hatch.

- You are astounded that the weight of grief is *unmatched* by anything you ever felt before when death takes your grandchild. Logic demands that since you are the older person, death should claim you first . . . surely not the child! Not the child that brought so much *pure* joy. You go about trying to accomplish the normal routine tasks of life. You fulfill your obligations to family, friends, and employees. You manage somehow to carry out your duties and you look as if you are coping and have it all pulled together; but the name of that dear child lies *unspoken* on your tongue and hovers there *unwanted* in the edges of all your thoughts. Others, insensitive to your rawness, sandpaper your wounds with the smallness of their talk. Your turmoil is *unstilled* and your heart left *uncomforted*. Your emotions are smashed into a million pieces and you feel they will always *be unmendable*.

- You learn from a series of doctors that the illness afflicting you or someone you love is *untreatable*. They say, "You'll have to learn to live with this." Whatever that means! Maybe you have just been given the most shocking news imaginable, as was this forty-one-year-old woman, who wrote,

Today, my doctor said that after taking all the tests I have

---

*People Magazine, May 9, 1987.

taken, he feels that I could have Alzheimer's disease. I had to look it up in the medical guide to even know how to spell it. I really can't say how I feel except I'm filled with sheer fear.

It is easy to relate to her fears. But, in the meantime—somewhere between learning to live with it and the destructiveness of the disease itself—the fears, mental suffering, and anxieties are completely *unbearable*. After what you have already experienced and *undergone*, you are sure that one day soon you'll cross the line of sanity, and your mind will crack and you or your loved one will be lost forever.

• You have buried the most searing memories of some long ago child abuse or neglect, preferring to not deal with the pain. Yet, *unbidden*, some traumatic incident or *unwanted* confrontation ignites the flame of your forgotten horrors and your past *undeniably* burns its way into your present. The memory of that childhood abuse now triggers off a horrible war within you. The pain is all fresh, the dirty feeling revived, and the poor self-image concept seems locked in.

You go to ridiculous lengths to get the approval of others. You try to attach yourself to a "good" person in the mistaken hope that somehow the goodness of another will rub off on you, making your "badness" disappear. You experience many death wishes because you feel so *unclean* and *unaccepted* by others.

• You have the kind of marriage that appears to be picture perfect and strong enough to remain *undissolvable*. The marriage, to the outsider or even to someone in the family, looks *undisputably* healthy. It appears to be a growing, thriving union full of life; but, in reality, the marriage is frail and ailing. Perhaps, even from its beginning, it was a wrong choice and has been dead for many years. Only the pretense and elaborate masquerade which was carefully cultivated around the marriage has kept it alive. In reality, all is gone. Now differences between you and your mate are *unreconcilable* unless there is some God-inspired miracle to hold you together. The *unpronounceable* word "divorce" becomes a real life occurrence for you, and the stigma of *uncoupling* a hell that even in your wildest nightmares was *unforeseen*. Especially for Christian couples. In fact, you would feel as this former pastor's wife—

> The day I signed the divorce papers was the worst day of my life. I was *unloved, unwanted, unfit, unusable,* and mostly *unchristian.*

or, the pastor who wrote—

> A word about me—Ten years ago, I went through a divorce. My world caved in on me. I was a pastor. I thought my life and ministry were over. I didn't want to kill myself, but I did feel like dying.
>
> I know hundreds of preachers from college and seminary days—but only one called to ask, "Can I help?"
>
> My own family turned on me. I was accused of not being a Christian, not being saved, and some suggested demon possession.
>
> I didn't argue. I didn't try to explain, I just remained silent and hurt. I did drive up I-95 at 3:00 in the morning screaming at the top of my lungs because of the pain I felt. I felt *unwanted, unloved, unimportant,* and *unnecessary.* I felt all the good I had ever done was down the drain.

When any of the unworld ordeals come into our lives we, like the woman and pastor above, are faced with an issue we'd rather not deal with or confess. However, the plain truth is— we have to decide, How important is it—to us—to survive?

This decision-making time comes during the most crucial moments of our lives. The choice to live or die is not made quickly or flippantly. We come to survival choices only after we have wrestled long and hard, as Jacob did with the angel of

God. We struggle, we search, and we thoroughly examine the intentions of our inner soul.

I am by no means suggesting that taking one's life is *ever* a good or acceptable thing to do . . . for it irrevocably destroys all options. I *am* talking about the terrible reality one goes through mentally, emotionally, and spiritually when consumed by suicidal feelings.

The making of this choice brings us into our own personal garden of Gethsemane, and we do not enter or leave it casually; but we sweat, as it were, blood and tears because of the turmoil, the people, and the conflicts involved. We are all too aware of the responsibility we take on when we make these choices, so we make them with deliberate forethought tempered by our love and fear of God. We don't look at it as a suicide, in the strictest terms, but rather as a very desperate act to leave the incredible pain of our existence. Dying becomes a welcome escape, a relief, and a means of *losing* our pain.

Yet, when our choice or decision becomes known to our family, friends, and associates, we are stunned by some of the *unbelievable* and *uncharitable* responses.

The icy rejection of others' responses, to our wanting to leave the pain of our lives, makes us feel *unworthy* of any calling we may have felt we had. Some see us, but choose to pretend that we do not exist; so we feel invisible. Others are openly outraged or righteously indignant about our proposed decision to end our life, or our other alternatives, and choose to point the finger of accusation. They stone us with their indictments and so we become convinced that we are *unholy* and *unusable* by God or mankind.

Still others—again, because of the survival choice we have made—declare us *unfit* to be around as though we have a contagious disease. So they walk away from us, leaving us quarantined in the misery of the leper's camp—*untouched* and *unattended*.

And sometimes the thundering loud voices of our Christian brothers and sisters shriek so harshly about us that we cannot hear the still small voice of God's Spirit. As one Christian leader sadly concluded, "The ABCs of the body of Christ toward a hurting brother or sister are

Accuse
Blame
Criticize."

Soon we believe that the choice we've made is a sin and an *unforgivable* one at that.

We feel victimized, assassinated, or banished from the caring body of believers by those who choose to play the role of God in *our* unworld crisis. These self-appointed vicars of God are *unmerciful* in their judgments, *unrestrained* in their verbal criticisms, and *unrelenting* in their pursuit of those who differ from their personal theology or their own biblical interpretation. (And God help us if they truly or mistakenly find a way to attach any kind of sexual sin to our lives.)

These crusaders, on white horses, stay on a constant alert, ready to defend God and His children (as if God needs it) and seem eager to purge any *highly visible* sinners within the congregation, be they the minister or director of music, the Sunday School teacher, the organist, or the church secretary.

Pastors, authors, or leaders in the church at large or involved in a radio or television ministry are particularly vulnerable. The critics' vindicating swords are the quickest to cut out the "cancer" in Christian leadership. The flaws, the weaknesses, the mistakes, the failures, and, most of all, the transgressions of others are almost gleefully pointed out for "We must get the sin out of the pulpit!" (to borrow the words of a well-known leader).

Yet, all the while these avengers of God ride, they breathe a sigh of relief that (at least for another day) their *own* secret sins or their emotional struggles are still *unknown*, still safe in their hiding places, and still *undiscovered*. Even if they believe with all their hearts that murder is a sin, they do not hesitate a moment to verbally annihilate and assassinate another's personhood, calling it expedient and justifiable to the cause of Christ.

The actions of these crusaders clearly illustrate exactly the reverse of New Testament love. I have found that if our self-appointed critics' swords slash us in too many places, and if our wounds are multiplied, then eventually we are too bloody and too broken to move. We lie down, we give up, and we lose the ability to care about going on. We watch life ebb slowly out of us; and, even if a godly, caring person comes along and does try to bind up our broken hearts and spirit, we are so far gone that we feel our personhood is *unnecessary*, our work *unwanted*, and all our life's efforts *unvalid*. We feel *undone*, as though the hand of God has lifted off our shoulders; and, in the end, we feel *uncalled*.

Perhaps you're thinking that I've overreacted or done an overkill job on the unworld process, but I think not. I've talked with thousands of people (at my speaking engagements) in the last year, and have read several hundred letters each month—all from people who are presently in the unworld agony. Therefore, I believe that I've not exaggerated the extent of the brokenness I see around me in our world today.

And since I've so recently experienced one of the most painful of all unworld circumstances, I write out of an ever-expanding vortex of truth.

We are bound together, you and I, in much the same manner as I earlier described the women prisoners and the families of the patients in the hospital waiting room. We all wait together, trying to make sense out of our ordeal, trying to cope with the crisis of the moment, trying to persevere in spite of the shattering brokenness of our experience, trying to find some meaning in our suffering, and trying somehow to find our way back into wholeness and hope once more.

The Un-Feeling — 1984-1986

Unwanted
Unusable
Unimportant
Unnecessary
Unworthy
Unforgivable
Unpardonable
Unacceptable
Uneffective
Unqualified
Unclean
Unholy
Unloved

—Joyce Landorf Heatherley

3

I am certainly not the first writer to pen my thoughts, experiences, feelings, and responses about the unworld episodes of our lives—nor will I be the last. These unworld tragedies have happened down through the centuries and will continue in the future, so there will always be a writer somewhere, at home or in exile, perhaps even in prison . . . writing, recording, or journalizing those events. Someone will always retell their unbelievable unworld story.

History proves that whether the story is told in Egyptian hieroglyphics painted in Egyptian tombs, scratched on bits of broken pottery shards, quill-penned on parchment paper or skins, etched on catacomb walls in Rome, typed on paper, captured on film, broadcast over the airwaves, shown on television, or printed out from a computer disk . . . the story *will* be told! For who can resist plot lines when they are so shocking, so intimate, and so foreign to anything we've ever seen or felt before? The unworld text can penetrate our minds and hearts like some elusive cat burglar who, in the dead of night, invades the most heavily guarded rooms of our lives and blatantly, without a pang of regret, steals our dearest and most precious treasures—shattering our inner peace and producing our deepest wounds. Actually, I believe unworld issues are faithfully chronicled lest we forget their important lessons.

I am grateful for the legions of unworld writers before me who have deliberately kept records of their agonies for us to read and to gain not only knowledge but wisdom as well. I personally believe that when they gain enough courage and strength to write, the ink from their pens is strong, even three-fold strong—if not more. I feel an author's recounting of his or her life's events are invaluable for us—currently broken and stunned with our own trauma.

In the first place, I think we need to read about the grievous journeys of others so we will be encouraged and motivated to remember that when out lives are swept into unworld agony we are not to subscribe to the idea that God, by some weird or whimsical quirk in His personality, has singled us out for cruel and unusual punishment. Nor has He forsaken us or dumped us like some decaying piece of useless garbage in an obscure alley trash can. Indeed, our loving heavenly Father does not abandon us, leaving us to call sarcastically over His shoulder, "Now, you shape up or ship out!" *Cruel* and *sadistic* are not words which describe the characteristics of the God we love and serve. So I believe it will help to know that when this unthinkable journey happens, and we struggle to crawl through this treacherous valley of the wounded, we *will* . . . like others before us, and those who will follow after us . . . come through the valley and out the other side. It's called survival.

Secondly, we need to read the accounts of others so we will be able, though pain constricts our vision, to see in illustration after illustration how beautifully God and His people can work together touching lives for good, not evil. Then we'll be able to watch for meaning and fulfillment as they are brought into our own fragile, suffering souls.

And, thirdly, we need to read about the unworld lessons learned by others so our hope will be restored. I have found that under ordinary everyday stress, or even when dealing with common painful disappointments of life, we clutch hope to our bosoms longer than any other single feeling. We hang on to hope, trust in hope, and even cherish the hope which seems to be rooted in our souls. However, with the explosion of an unworld event, the devastation is often so complete that hope, almost in an instant, begins to evaporate away. In fact, in far less time than it takes to write out this sentence, we can come directly to a place where our hope dries up, and our dreams wither and fade away. Ultimately, without the life-sustaining nutrients of hope in our system, our will to live and our want to go on (which are barely holding on by their fingertips) loosen their grips, fall, and die alongside of hope.

From the beginning of time, the unvarnished reality and truth of the unworld's trauma, and the torture which always accompanies it, has been passed down to people through every age and every century—missing no culture and no race of people.

Even starting in Genesis, the first book of the Old Testament—and right on through the New Testament—the travail of unworld people is chronicled.

I believe that while we don't know all the details about Adam and Eve, or too much of their early years as husband and wife after they were banished from the garden of Eden, still we do know them well enough to make some observations and comparisons. It's not too hard to see that they were probably the first in a long stream of humanity to discover, to their unbelievable horror, the despair and confusion of the unworld tragedy.

We can identify with this first unworld couple and feel the wounding process that Adam and Eve must have endured when the unthinkable thing, which had *never* happened before, now happens. *One son is killed.* While the shocking horror is slashing and piercing the parents' hearts, their unworld experience is compounded by a second fact. *Another son is the killer.* The two enormous unworld disasters converge on each other, and we can only try to imagine their feelings of guilt, despair, rage, and grief.

Often I've pictured a series of scenes in my head about the moment of Adam and Eve's unworld horror. In the book, *He Began With Eve,* I fictionalized those scenes on paper. I see it happening like this:

At night, by their tent's cooking fire, Adam and Eve instructed their children with their continual telling and retelling of their beginnings and their earlier existence with God. Whether they were training their children properly or succeeding at parenting, they could never be completely sure. Neither of these first parents had any memories to draw upon. No childhood memories of mother, father, brothers, or sisters; and no comparisons or conclusions could be formed from their past heritages. They simply lived and spoke what they felt God wanted them to do in the nurturing of their children.

However, they seriously doubted their parenting skills one harvest time, some thirty or so years after they had begun their family. They were stunned and shaken to the core of their beings by their first devastating tragedy.

That particular harvest season, both Cain and Abel brought forth their offerings for God as Adam and Eve had taught them. Cain's offering was made up of fruits and vegetables from his farm while Abel's was his newest and fattest lamb. Adam and Eve never foresaw that God would reject Cain's produce and accept Abel's lamb.

Eve was working with several of her daughters, drying wooly sheepskins for clothing, when one of the younger boys came running and screaming across the open field. When the child caught his wind and spoke his message, Eve could only stare, open-mouthed at her young son. Cain had committed a horrific deed against his brother, Abel.

Running across a clearing and a newly planted field, Eve

frantically searched for her husband. When she found him, she gave him the bare essentials, for that was all she knew, and then she blurted out, "We fed Cain and Abel the same porridge. They slept in the same tents. We loved them both in their own individual ways. Why did Cain kill his brother? Why?"

On into the night these questions raged in Eve's mind. By the cold, early dawn's light, her mind had quieted, and she was now kneeling by Abel's stiffened body when Adam, looking out across the field, said, "Eve . . . Cain comes."

Eve rose up and slowly walked out to meet him. When she was within touching distance, she flung her words at him.

"You had no right to do this bloody deed. How *dare* you wrench the life out of your brother?" She went on and on with her accusations, her voice burning deeply into Cain's conscience. Then, before he could defend himself or reply, Eve sensed the answer within her.

"The serpent! Was the serpent there?" she asked.

"No," Cain's barely audible voice responded. "I was by myself. I alone am guilty."

"But I don't understand why! Why did you . . . do this?" Eve looked back up the hill at the mound which was Abel's lifeless body.

"I was angry at God," Cain's defense began. "He would not accept my offering, but he willingly received Abel's. My anger and hatred for both God and Abel took hold of me and so I . . . I . . . did this thing."

Eve looked at the hardening lines of rebellion around Cain's eyes and instantly saw a reflection of her own day of disobedience. She was painfully stabbed with the memory that remained of her own devastating actions. The inner wounds had not healed.

Then, in a voice so low Eve had to bend forward to hear, Cain described his conversation with God which had occurred immediately after he'd killed his brother. In a flat monotone voice, drained of emotion, Cain related God's words and ended by telling his mother of the bargain struck between them insuring his physical safety.

Eve was not soothed nor did Cain's words help her through the quagmire of her grief. Bitter were the thoughts which welled up in her heart as she remembered the day God had asked the question, . . . "Where is your brother?" then aloud, she wailed, "Oh what a waste! This wretched life is all sorrow."

Even in today's culture—with our media-conscious familiarity with crime and vice squads, killings and hideous torture, criminals and victims, and unspeakable atrocities—we, like Adam and Eve, are never ready for unworld fatalities. I think we can't be prepared to handle the paralyzing grief and pain when, in an instant, it reaches inside our home and wrenches the life out of one of our own family. Consequently, again, like those first parents of so long ago, we stare in disbelief at the cold facts before us, when it is *our* son, *our* daughter, *our* wife, *our* husband . . . and the shattering process is authentic and unbearable, just as it must have been for Adam and Eve.

How amazing that God allows us to view His chosen people on the pages of the Bible, not only during their high and holy times when they are practically dancing in the streets, ebullient with joy and ready to burst with their successes, but also when they cower in some dark corner covered with the repugnant odor of failure and despair. Take the prophet Elijah, for example. Even though the great man of God was fresh from his glorious and incredible victories, he sat down under a bush and prayed that he'd die. It's as if God parts the private curtains of His people's souls and we are able to see them in both their joy and in their most naked and vulnerable states. God carefully registers their dark thoughts and even darker questions, their public and their private sins, their serious weaknesses and their various flaws, and their brick wall denial or their vulnerable acceptance of their unworld catastrophe.

How grateful I am that, within the pages of Scripture, God has written a document of truth about His people . . . revealing both the good and the bad. It seems to me God didn't want us to cultivate a fairy tale ambience about our lives—a fantasy story that implies once we have come to Him, we will be wonderfully happy ever after. Instead He chose to teach us truth when He gave us real world portraits of men and women living life *not* as they wanted or fantasized it to be, but as it *really* was. His apparent message was intended for our good so we would not live out our lives under imaginary or false delusions. God knew that life is difficult enough without endlessly spinning our wheels of energy in pursuit of a dead end.

Across the pages of the Bible march countless men and women who were plagued by the unworld process, yet who survived and who were dearly loved by God.

Moses was one such person. As a newborn, he escaped the Egyptian pharaoh's death order for all Hebrew male babies because of his mother's incredible scheme. Jochebed placed him in a basket and floated him in the reeds and tall grasses on the edge of the Nile River. Soon after, the infant was rescued by one of Pharaoh's daughters and then adopted as her son. Moses grew up enjoying, and accustomed to, the privileges and education afforded royalty.

When he became a man, Moses became acutely aware of the slavery and the terrible conditions of his people, the Hebrews; and, losing control, he lashed out and deliberately murdered an Egyptian. Then, for the second time, he escaped death at the hands of Pharaoh by fleeing to the desert. He had begun his unworld ordeal.

One can only wonder how Moses rationalized his tending the sheep of his father-in-law in view of his amazing background and privileged upbringing of his former life. How in the world did he go from enjoying the pampered status of Egyptian prince to which he was accustomed—with all its luxurious ways: its finely prepared and delicious dinners and banquets, its exquisitely embroidered and impeccably laundered linen clothing, its love and almost worship of bathing and cleanliness, its work and play times always designed to stretch one's mind—to a life as a lonely Hebrew shepherd on a barren desert?

We may never know how Moses adjusted or accepted being a dirty, unkempt, smelly shepherd who ate whatever meager amounts of goats' milk cheese and bread available, whose mind was endlessly bored with the job, and who rarely had the opportunity to bathe or change his clothes. But he *did* manage to survive!

It's my guess that just about the time Moses adjusted to his obscure life as a shepherd in the desert and had somehow made his peace about the man he killed . . . God chose that exact moment to intervene and change Moses' destiny by appearing in a burning bush.

We see this shepherd listening as God compassionately outlines the sorrows and the oppression of the Hebrews in Egypt. Moses is nodding his head in knowledgeable agreement, for what he's hearing is well known and true. But then God explains that His solution for the delivery and restoration of His people is a man named Moses; and it is safe to assume the man didn't take it very well.

Now I can see Moses, in my mind's eye, as he leans a little closer in towards the fiery bush, his mind positively choking with fear, and he thinks, almost aloud: "This is *unreal!* After living in the barren desert for these years and after what I've been through at the hands of the Egyptians, if God thinks I'm going *back* there, He's got another 'think' coming! There's no way I'm going to be that stupid . . . they'll kill me for sure. No, sir, not Egypt. No disrespect, God, but no, no, no thank you!"

The Bible relates the whole story and how, indeed, Moses was God's finely tuned instrument. But think for a moment, how unreal, improbable, and unthinkable it all must have sounded to this former Egyptian prince of remarkable birth and heritage who had escaped Egypt with his life and for forty years had been a rather ordinary Hebrew sheep tender. Anyone who has ever lost a job, lost their esteem and respect from others, lost a calling somewhere in the valley of despair, or has lost the visions or dreams for the future—has stood in the shepherd sandals of Moses, knowing that the past's sins, questions, and doubts would have to remain unexplained. And most of us reading the remarkable encounter Moses had with God, would wish, *just once*, God would appear to us in a burning bush and tell us what way we should go and what we should do as graphically as He did for Moses!

Then there's the minor prophet, Habakkuk. Listen to his heart as he spews out an angry prayer to God about the unworld unfairness in the courts, the unethical practices of others, and the undeniable sin of murder going on in his time.

O Lord, how long must I call for help before you will listen? I shout to you in vain; there is no answer. "Help! Murder!" I cry, but no one comes to save. Must I forever see this sin and sadness all around me?

Wherever I look, there is oppression and bribery and men who love to argue and fight. The law is not enforced and there is no justice given in the courts, for the wicked far outnumber the righteous and bribes and trickery prevail.

Oh Lord my God, my Holy One, you who are eternal—is your plan in all of this to wipe us out? Surely not!*

We are one with Habakkuk; we know his face, we hear his cry of outrage, and we share his fury.

I could go on, giving Old Testament examples of people

---

*Hebrews 1:2–4, 12, *The Living Bible*.

who came face to face with unworld occurrences, but let me move on to a few New Testament people. Undoubtedly, I'll miss a great many, and I suspect that there were other biblical unworld people and tragedies that went unrecorded. But consider some of these men and women.

There is the mother of Mary . . . who became the grandmother of Jesus.

She is called Hannah in Marjorie Holmes's very moving novel, *Two From Galilee,* and we are given a graphic glimpse of the unworld which exploded around Mary and her parents, Hannah and Joachim. I've read this remarkable book several times and it always put me in the very special position of seeing and reacting to Mary as I might have responded to my own daughter.

Hannah must have felt the weight of all the anguish in the world when her beautiful, exquisite daughter, Mary—who is engaged to Joseph—tries to calmly say: "Mother, I must tell you. It has been three months now since my loins have bled." Hannah's face is described as a "face that fell suddenly, as if a blow had struck it, then slowly drained."

We can see the paralyzing effect of the news on Hannah. How devastating all that must have sounded. Put yourself in Hannah's place as you read this excerpt about Hannah's unworld moment:

> Hannah had been sitting with her eyes shut. Now she opened them and gazed a long moment at her daughter. "Yes, Mary, I believe you," she said. "Heaven knows if I didn't! . . ." She shuddered and shut her eyes once more, as if to escape it. The disgrace. After all her boasting. If now, on top of the humiliation of stepping down, there were to be no proper wedding, but merely a shamed public acknowledgement that the marriage had been consummated in secret—legal as that was, it was still ignoble, degrading. People sneered and made contemptuous jests. No, no. She had been punished enough for

her vainglorious claims; God was surely going to spare her this.

. . . These fantastic thoughts lashed through Hannah as she sat trying to regain her composure, her command of the day. The devils were battering at her again: how much do we really know of those close to us, they asked? How much does even the most careful mother know about her child? Look at her, this beautiful small daughter standing before you, a very princess, alien to all you ever were. She harbors a secret still. She is rich and full with a secret thing.

And the devils whipped their tails and screamed: "Adultery means death by stoning! Shame, divorce, death." Even if a man had pounced on her out of the hedges as she came home one night from the meadows, she would be sullied, defiled. Even Joseph would not have her; no man would. . . . Hannah saw her beloved crouching, begging for mercy, heard the stones raining down. She saw the white body bruised and bleeding, perhaps hurled over a cliff. . . .

Hannah sprang up, grabbing at the garments to be plunged into the steaming tub. She must scrub them and cleanse them and spread them out in God's clean thirsty sun. She must again grasp the garments of life and force them into patterns of neatness and precision. What folly to sit wasting time over nothing.

"Come now, let's get busy," she said. I'll make you a potion that will make your blood flow once more. But first we must finish the washing."

"Mother, wait," Mary reached out a restraining hand. "You had better sit down again. There is something more that I have to tell you. And this—this I fear will be even harder for you to believe."

One can only guess at the depths of Hannah's pain or at the high levels of emotional woe she must have endured. And like some unworld events which are not only unbearable but unmentionable as well, we can only wonder who could this about-to-be grandmother tell? Who would understand it? I suspect it was a stigma that Hannah, or whatever her real name was, was never able to shed. Perhaps she was forever shunned by the other women who drew water at the common well, and forever felt the cold fog of invisibility as it hung on her like a dark shroud. One thing I'm sure of: She was never the same after that unworld day.

And what of the compounded events of John the Baptist's unworld experience? John, who had a dramatic miraculous birth. Everyone knew the story about his older and barren parents, Elizabeth and Zacharias. It was an oft told tale of how an angel of God promised them a son and made great predictions about that son, going so far as to compare John's character and spirit to that of the prophet Elijah.

John was a specially called man of God, and lived up to his angelic advanced notices. He dedicated his life to one cause and one cause only: to preach repentance, baptism, and the coming of his cousin Jesus, the Messiah. His single-mindedness to God's call and fulfilling his own destiny was simply awesome. John's fervent love for God could not be diminished and his motives and heart's intent were never in question. He was an intense and driven man who knew exactly where he would go and what he would say. The people of the day heard him proclaim his mission statement the length and breadth of the land. Many, many believed his message and became his followers and disciples.

It was John who baptized Jesus at the Jordan River and, as if he needed any proof of Christ's identity or God's seal of approval on the baptism, all those present, including John, heard the voice of the Spirit of God coming down from heaven saying, "This is my beloved Son, and I am wonderfully pleased with him."*

It's hard to envision this self-assured, brave, and coura-

---

*Matthew 3:17, *The Living Bible.*

46

geous man, John, a few months later in prison. From what we read in Matthew 11 and Luke 7:18, he was probably questioning the veracity of his calling and he must have been troubled and doubting his own words about the authenticity of Jesus. Evidently he had heard about Jesus' miracles and preaching, and he had a serious struggle with it all. We are told that John instructed his own disciples to go to Jesus and ask, "Are you really the one we are waiting for, or shall we keep looking?"*

The unspoken questions smoldering in John's heart must have been: "If you are *not* the Messiah, then who are you? Have I wasted my life?" Also, "If you *are* the true Messiah, the King of Israel, the one I was told would come, why don't you overthrow the wicked government, bring peace, and establish your rightful kingdom, as the prophets foretold?" And, of course, the most fiery question that simply had to burn deeply into John's mind would have been, "Jesus, if you are able to do all these miracles I keep hearing about, why do you leave me in chains here in Herod's prison? Aren't you my own cousin, if not the Messiah? I don't understand. Why don't you rescue me?"

I am confident that John rarely, if ever, questioned or doubted his God-calling while he was growing up or struggling for existence on the desert prior to his public ministry. It probably never crossed his mind, in those days, to wonder if he were called by God to be what the scriptures call the forerunner of Christ. But later, in prison, I feel John's unworld experience produced a difficult, hard-to-believe series of problems; and who knows what he thought, felt or believed in those days just prior to his death.

Just today as I was reading the mail, it was as though I heard the echoes of the enigma John the Baptist faced so long ago. I heard them most strongly when I read a letter from a

---

*Matthew 11:2, 3, *The Living Bible*.

friend, a young dentist I've known for some eight or nine years now. In his letter, Abe tells me that he believed God called him into the profession of dentistry several years back, and he thanks me for my part in sustaining him through the difficulty of dental school. But now that he is a dentist, almost finished with the military service and about to go into private practice, he is feeling the pressures of the unexpected and the unknown. He wonders in his letter what the Lord really wants of him. I can see some parallels, in my present day friend and John of the New Testament, with their questions and doubts. Especially when my friend writes of those *past* years and says,

> I was a little more certain *then* than now as to how the Lord wants me to use my talents and degree. Your prayers are appreciated.

While circumstances of John and my friend are centuries apart, and certainly Abe is not facing death, still the *unknown* anxieties and fears are present within both men . . . perhaps with even the same or similar questions and doubts.

John was deep into his unworld, unbelievable experience. He probably couldn't make any sense out of it. It must have been unthinkable to him that Jesus would deliberately let him waste away in prison. John's last days and nights in prison must have been spent in total anguish and in the most realistic dungeons of unworld horror. We can sense his inconsolable feelings of betrayal, of abandonment, and of his crushed spirit. It would not be unrealistic to imagine that perhaps, as he knelt over the beheading block, he died weeping with despair, thinking that his life's whole purpose stood for nothing except to mock him. Unthinkable!

There was also Stephen, one of seven deacons appointed to serve in the early church at Jerusalem. How did he feel when he innocently voiced his convictions about the breach between Jewish tradition, temple cults, and the new faith taught by Jesus, only to find himself charged with blasphemy against God and Moses by the authorities in the Sanhedrin? And, what were his thoughts when, after he presented his eloquent and brilliant defense, he was sentenced to death by stoning?

We know that God gave Stephen special dying grace and must have filled his soul with the acceptance and unbelievable peace which passes all understanding ... but what did he think in between the trial and the time of his death? We can only guess. Stephen might never have dreamed his theological apologetics would bring about his death, yet he went through his unworld experience with enormous grace; and, in spite of his words and the unbelievable outcome of his life, we still hear the echoes of the young Stephen's teachings as they are passed down through the generations and centuries for all of us to read in the book of Hebrews.

And what of the man who held the coat of Stephen as he was killed by stoning? The man who "was in hearty agreement with the killing of Stephen." The man who was described as "a wild man, going everywhere to devastate believers, even entering private homes and dragging out men and women alike and jailing them."*

That same man who, after his remarkable conversion to Christ on the road to Damascus, was convinced that God wanted him to preach the gospel among the Jews and Gentiles. This man, once named Saul and then renamed by God as Paul, was totally transformed—no more did he threaten with every breath to destroy the small body of believers. Instead, he immediately began preaching the good news in Damascus.

Like so many of us, it is doubtful that Paul was prepared for his unworld experience. For how was Paul to guess that

*Acts 8:1, 3, *The Living Bible.*

the more fervently he preached about Jesus being the Christ, the more the Jewish leaders conspired to kill him, doing to him just as he had once done to the believers? At one point, Paul—after preaching, and to escape being killed—had to be let down in a basket through an opening in the city wall. Then in Jerusalem, almost every time he tried to serve God by sharing his newfound faith, the same thing happened; his life was in mortal danger. So the converts of the early church decided it was best to send him home to Tarsus for his own safety.

At this point, Paul's life story enters into what the biblical commentaries call "The Silent Years." Could it be that after his dramatic conversion and call to preach, the most unthinkable thing began to happen? I believe so. Paul must have been stunned to realize that he was rejected by the same Jews that he once conspired with against Christians; and quite quickly he found that, if he wasn't very security conscious, his preaching was going to cost him his life. How unthinkable that must have been—after his conversion, after his knowing that the call of God on his life was *to preach*, and after he had forsaken his former obsession with persecuting Christians. Now Paul finds his life is in constant jeopardy, and he continually has to seek methods of escaping his assassins!

Those "Silent Years" after his conversion consume a considerable period of time—as many as ten to twelve years. We don't know too much about this time in Paul's life, and of course that has prompted many speculations and questions which have persisted through the centuries.

What we *do* know is that Paul did not talk or write about two very important issues in his life: He never addressed the whys and wherefores of his "Silent Years" exile; nor did he ever spell out the details of his "thorn in the flesh." This latter issue has been the basis of a veritable storm of conjecture by church leaders, lay people, and theologians for a long time.

The most hotly debated point was the question of what *was*, exactly, Paul's "thorn." But, I have wondered something else: Why would such an outspoken and honest man like Paul keep the nature of his "thorn" a secret, even carrying it to his grave? Apparently he didn't reveal the answer to anyone. Why couldn't Paul share this unworld experience? Could it be that both his exile and his thorn were so hideous and so *unthinkable* to Paul that, even with his brilliant mind and exceptional oratory skills, he found those two experiences were *unspeakable*?

It is my guess that the dark unworld memories stabbed away at him for his entire lifetime. Those ordeals too painful to be dealt with publicly, unbearable, so much so, that being cold, sick, hungry, shipwrecked, stoned and left for dead, old, or imprisoned, paled away to nothing in the light of the "Silent Years" and the "thorn." Gifted as he was, and as committed to being open and transparent with the early church he loved . . . still Paul left his terrible unworld issues . . . unwritten. What cheers my heart and strengthens my faith is that, in spite of Paul's unworld memories, God used him in spectacular ways and Paul survived with much class and much grace!

There was also Peter. Here was a man who was as much remembered for his betrayal of Christ as for his being the rock or foundation of the first century church. I suspect that no one knew better than Peter himself that his unworld experience started unfolding right after he and the other disciples had met in the upper room with Jesus and had partaken of the first sacramental communion.

The New Testament book of Mark reveals that after they sang a hymn, they went out to the Mount of Olives, and it was there Jesus predicted, " 'All of you will desert me. . . .'

"Peter said to him, 'I will never desert you no matter what the others do!'

" 'Peter,' Jesus said, 'before the cock crows a second time

tomorrow morning, you will deny me three times.'

" 'No!' Peter exploded. 'Not even if I have to die with you! I'll *never* deny you!' And all the others vowed the same."*

Peter was still arrogant with loyalty later in the olive grove. And when the squad of soldiers, police, and high priest servants came to arrest Jesus, it was Peter (as John tells it) who cut off the servant's ear with his sharpened, ready sword. Then Peter's unworld experience, like an ugly boil, came rapidly to a head.

A servant girl recognized him and declared that he was one of those with Jesus. Vehemently, he denied it. Then someone else looked closely at Peter and declared, "You must be one of them." Again, he claimed he was not! Finally, someone else identified Peter as a disciple of Jesus; and Peter, cursing angrily, denied it for the third time just as the rooster crowed.

"At that moment Jesus turned and looked at Peter. Then Peter remembered what he had said—'Before the rooster crows tomorrow morning, you will deny me three times.' "

"And Peter walked out of the courtyard, crying bitterly."**

Peter's world was now cut open; he was exposed for all to see. He had fulfilled Christ's prediction; he had done the unthinkable. He was now unusable, unholy, and an unwanted disciple of Christ. No wonder he wept bitterly.

Somehow, if I've ever wanted to write anything quite so emphatically . . . it is this. Think, just think, what Peter— after the crucifixion and resurrection of Christ—must have been feeling about himself, his disgraceful past, *and* his chances of being used by God in the future.

He must have thought, or at least surmised, that because

---

*Mark 14:27, 29–31, *The Living Bible*.
**Luke 22:61, 62, *The Living Bible*.

of his denial of his Lord, he would never again be useful to bring about the kingdom of God. He certainly would have considered that his future job would revert back to his former occupation—that of being a fisherman.

Yet that was not the way it was to be . . . evidently God is never handicapped by what we think are endings. Perhaps when we, like Peter, feel most unusable, that's God's best opportunity to make the most of new beginnings.

Space and time do not permit me to speculate on the unworld events encountered by all the great men and women of the Bible, but I can hardly omit the one whose person, life, and mission are the subject of the whole New Testament: Jesus. I dare not be presumptuous enough to think that I can pinpoint our Lord's unworld moments. Nor can I say for certain that He even *had* an unworld, unthinkable ordeal . . . however,

> For since he himself has now been through suffering and temptation, he knows what it is like when we suffer and are tempted, and he is wonderfully able to help us.*
> For ours is not a High Priest who cannot sympathize with our weaknesses, but One who was in every respect tested as we are, yet without committing any sin.**

My logic is that since these scriptures say Jesus did know what suffering and temptation were all about, then He must have experienced the human dilemma of the unworld's grievous agony.

It seems to me one of the unworld ordeals which haunted Jesus all through his life was the circumstances of His birth and the speculation, privately or publicly, about his illegitimacy.

Twice Jesus went back to His hometown of Nazareth, and each time He was ridiculed and rejected. One can almost hear

---

* Hebrews 2:18, *The Living Bible.*
**Hebrews 4:15, *Modern Language Bible.*

the scorn in the voices of His very own people in Nazareth in Mark's account of the last time Jesus was preaching in Nazareth. We read,

> Soon afterwards he left that section of the country and returned with his disciples to Nazareth, his hometown. The next Sabbath he went to the synagogue to teach, and the people were astonished at his wisdom and his miracles because he was just a local man like themselves.
>
> "He's no better than we are," they said. "He's just a carpenter, Mary's boy. . . ."*

The words "Mary's boy" were probably contemptuously spit out and were intended to hit as the rudest of all insults. Remember, by the cultural standards of the day, a man was usually described as the son of another man, such as "son of Joseph." To call Jesus "Mary's boy" was a more polite way of saying He was an illegitimate child—a bastard son.

In Jesus' short three-year ministry, it seems to me, His life had a series of unworld crisis points. As I reviewed and researched the events of Christ's life, in several biblical commentaries, I was struck by the number of times Jesus had to deal with who He was. He had an unworld identity problem. People tended to write Jesus off as someone's illegitimate son or they simply made Him invisible and ignored Him.

Here are a few of those events—Walk through the list, and feel our Lord's anguish and undoubted sense of frustration. Always, it seems, He was on trial, being rejected, criticized, or judged unfairly.

- Christ asks the disciples their opinions of Him
- Jesus begins now to predict His own death
- Jesus again predicts His own death

---

*Mark 6:1–3, *The Living Bible*.

- Jesus now claims to be the light of the world
- He announces Himself as a good shepherd
- He again calls Himself the Son of God
- Test questions before stoning of Jesus
- Jesus foretells His death a third time
- The Sanhedrists challenge His authority to teach
- The Sanhedrists sought to lay hands on Jesus
- Judas Iscariot conspires against Christ's life
- Jesus foretells and designates His betrayer
- Farewell words of Christ with His disciples
- Agony in Gethsemane
- Peter thrice denies that he knew the Lord
- Jesus avows that He is the Christ of God
  Herod and soldiers mock Jesus with robe, crown, and reed
- Jesus bears His cross
- He was crucified in the companionship of malefactors
- The jeers and gibes of enemies unto Christ
- His loud outcry of agony, "My God, My God, why have you forsaken me?"
- Having completed His sufferings, Jesus expired*

It was an *unthinkable* death for a man who did nothing but touch, heal, restore, and give life eternally to others. It is hard, terribly hard, to picture Jesus in his dying moments on a Roman crucifixion cross asking, even though His deity knew the answer, "My God, My God, why have you forsaken me?" But, I believe it does tell us that Jesus was not spared the human ordeal of unworld devastation.

What does all this say to us here and now? I choose to think that when Jesus suffered the ultimate of all unworld suffering in the crucifixion, it was one of the most graphic and powerful ways we can know that we are one with Him. It

---

*Merril F. Unger, *Unger's Bible Dictionary,* (Chicago: Moody Press, copyright © 1957).

is what Phillips Brooks once labeled a *shared experience*. He wrote,

> It is a strange thought to many, but it is a thought that grows very dear to the souls that really enter into it, that there was something in the crucifixion which it is our highest privilege to share.

We have a *shared experience* with Christ in our unworld tragedies. We are one with Him, the people of the Bible, and millions of other people who have survived unworld sufferings. The survivors and their experiences are real. They lived and died and others came along behind them. We belong to that invisible support group who have gone on since time began for humans.

Lately I have wondered what the disciples, and the small but rapidly growing band of Christians in the first century, would have thought had they known of the unthinkable, unholy carnage and unbelievable tortures to come? Could they, in their wildest imaginings, have foreseen the crusader holy wars from the ninth to the mid-fifteenth centuries? What would they have felt if they knew that, all in the name of their beloved Christ, such unworld terror would reign?

Who could have foreseen a woman like Joan of Arc (1412–1431) who, while in prison (and one month before her fiery death), affirmed her religious faith and said, "I am waiting on our Lord. I hold to what I've already said."

How could anyone imagine the frightening horrors of the Papal inquisitors and the Spanish inquisition? Those dreadful events which instigated and provoked writers and playwrights alike to see and deal with the unworld episodes of those times.

Today there is no way to watch a performance of *The Man of La Mancha*—a play taken from the writings of Cervantes about a hero of romance named Don Quixote—and be blind to the unworld echoes. Especially when Quixote admits that poets like himself are intrigued by madness because, as he explains to another prisoner, "Poets and madmen have much in common." While watching the play, we fear that madness will snap our minds as we are trying to make some sense and meaning out of life. Then we hear Don Quixote expound about his belief that poets and madmen both see life as it is. We are deeply moved by his stinging yet eloquent speech, when he tells about his "seeing life," unworld life . . . and we live his anguish as we listen to the outpouring of his soul as he impassionately speaks of seeing pain, misery, and cruelty beyond belief and of seeing life as it *really* is. Quixote's speech ends with a haunting question about death. He relates that in battle his dying comrades did not ask why they were dying . . . but why they had ever lived.

The unworld trauma is unthinkable and when its hell is unleashed in our lives, we can identify with Don Quixote. Readily we wonder why we have lived in the first place. Whether we are watching a play about the unworld trials of people during the Papal inquisition or reading letters of nineteenth century men and women, we see a common thread of unworld similarities and situations.

With a quick superficial glance, we think somehow that the sufferings of men and women in the recent past decades were unique to them and their generation, and have no voice of their own or no words of wisdom for us now, here in our unworld ordeal. But they do, oh how they do!

There was Hudson Taylor. He was the great pioneer missionary to China—a man whom we now revere, respect, and honor; and we are prone to believe, deny, or at least pretend that he didn't suffer as completely as history's previous unworld victims. But a study of his life shows that is not true.

While serving in China, Taylor lost not only his wife and his children, but his missionary co-workers as well. He suffered unbearable grief.

Hudson Taylor revealed his darkest despair, an emotion we would prefer to deny or set aside as minor and seldom felt for saints of God, in a letter to his mother. I am grateful that the contents of this letter were preserved for those of us ordinary Christians who have experienced despair and struggled with depression.

This great missionary reminded his mother that he had often asked her to remember him in her prayers. He stressed the importance of her praying for him by writing, "When I have done so [asked for her prayerful support], there has been much need of it." Then he goes on to add, "That need has never been greater than at present."

Then this renowned Christian leader, whom most of us think of and remember as nothing but victoriously successful, described the unworld persecution he was presently facing after years of consecrated work for God in China. His letter listed the responses of others toward him and the criticisms which were being leveled against him. Hudson Taylor's heartbreaking words jumped off the page as I read them. Oh, how this dear, dedicated, yet hurting saint of God must have despaired when he wrote,

Envied by some, despised by many, hated by others, often blamed for things I never heard of or had nothing to do with, an innovator on what have become established rules of missionary practice, an opponent of mighty systems of heathen error and superstition, working without precedent in many respects and with few experienced helpers, often sick in body as well as perplexed in mind and embarrassed by circumstances, had not the Lord been specially gracious to me, had not my mind been sustained by the conviction that the work is his and that he is with me in what it is no empty figure to call "the thick of the conflict," I must have fainted or broken down. But the battle is the Lord's and he will conquer. We may fail, do fail continually—but he never fails. Still, I need your prayers more than ever.*

Who of us can read about another's unworld moments and remain dry-eyed and unmoved or remain in denial about unworld ordeals even in the lives of famous, celebrated veterans of Christianity?

And who among us, who is old enough to remember, could forget exactly where we were when we heard the news of the bombing of Pearl Harbor, followed by United States President Franklin D. Roosevelt's announcement of our war with Japan? That bombing and the loss of lives, plus the unthinkable war which would follow, paralyzed us with the fear of the unknown that day.

For millions of Jewish people under the terror reign of Adolph Hitler, during that same war, the unworld holocaust came into being—annihilating whole families, their dreams, and their children's dreams. We have many records left documenting such unbelievable atrocities that we read them with a mixture of sorrowful belief and fearful unbelief. How did they endure? How did they find any meaning in life in the presence of such hideous suffering?

We read *The Diary of Anne Frank* or Corrie ten Boom's *The Hiding Place* and, even as we read, we shake our heads in dismay and in grief.

As I am writing these pages and reading them each night to my husband, he felt that I should be absorbing the life of the Vienna-born psychiatrist, Viktor E. Frankl. So yesterday, Francis bought me one of this incredibly sensitive and

Hudson Taylor's Spiritual Secret. Published by Moody Press

gifted man's books, *Man's Search for Meaning.**

Dr. Frankl writes out of his unworld experiences in the 1940s, during the holocaust years in Europe, when he was a prisoner being shuffled about from one concentration camp to another, including the dreaded camp at Auschwitz.

During his time in those bestial unworld concentration camps, Viktor Frankl lost every possession; his personal value was destroyed; he suffered from hunger, cold, and beatings; and, he expected to be exterminated every hour like some insignificant rodent or insect. He realized early into his unworld torture that he had "nothing to lose except his so ridiculously naked life."

Dr. Frankl's writings are so graphic and vivid that when reading the description of his life, and the lives of others, in the concentration camps, the very words seemed to rise up and off the pages.

As I read about his unworld ordeal, I tended to think that my experiences, my unworld traumas, were nothing; for they certainly pale significantly in comparison to Dr. Frankl's. I felt as if my unworld crises were insignificantly small and would never match the size and pain of others'. How could I say my unworld tragedy was as great as Jesus', or other biblical and historical figures from the past, or men and women who have had death camp battle scars like Viktor Frankl? My own trauma seemed almost trite and unnecessary to recount. I felt embarrassed to mention it, especially as the words of Dr. Frankl penetrated my soul . . . or when I looked into the pain-filled eyes of a fragile woman named Elsie. This precious elderly lady had survived a concentration camp, living as nothing but a number, and had lost everything. As I hugged her, I wondered what my suffering was, compared to hers?

Man's Search for Meaning, by Viktor E. Frankl. Copyright © 1959. Published by Washington Press.

As I was struggling with the fact that my unworld ordeal (or yours) may never match or parallel the suffering of others, Dr. Frankl gave an analogy that put things into a better perspective.

He told of man's suffering being similar to the behavior of gas. Then he recounted that, when you fill an empty chamber with a certain quantity of gas, the gas will fill the space in the chamber; and it will fill it evenly and completely . . . no matter how big or how small the chamber.

He went on to explain that suffering ". . . completely fills the human and conscious mind, no matter whether the suffering is great or little. There, the 'size' of human suffering is absolutely relative."

In other words, the extent or the intensity of the pain and brokenness we go through in our *own* unworld ordeal is not the issue here. Even if your unworld experience, or mine, could be described as of a lesser or greater intensity—it is only relative. For suffering, when it happens to you or to me, is just as devastating to us as anyone else because we personally are the *one enduring it.* Today's newspaper headline, *"New Drug May Help Alzheimer's Victims,"* will not touch or move us too much unless *yesterday* one of our loved ones was diagnosed as having Alzheimer's disease. Unworld suffering and pain fills each and every available space within us. The "equal" part is that suffering shatters everyone and is just as destructive to all.

I was struck by the author's note at the beginning of *The Gulag Archipelago,** when Aleksandr I. Solzhenitsyn wrote,

> For years I have with reluctant heart withheld from publication this already completed book: my obligation to those still living outweighed my obligation to the dead. But now that

---

**The Gulag Archipelago*, by Aleksandr I. Solzhenitsyn. Copyright © 1973. Published by Harper & Row Publishers, Inc.

State Security has seized the book anyway, I have no alternative but to publish it immediately.

In this book there are no fictitious persons, nor fictitious events. People and places are named with their own names. If they are identified by initials instead of names, it is for personal considerations. If they are not named at all, it is only because human memory has failed to preserve their names. But it all took place just as it is here described.

Somehow the unworld events of our lives must be told—as painful as they might be—for to tell only the lovely side of our lives, only the obvious success stories, only the "they lived happily ever after" tales, would not be reality. It would give a distorted picture of the truth about our existence, from Adam and Eve on down to our present existence.

I do not want to write or contribute any phony, hypocritical or deceptive words here; but, at the same time, neither do I want to communicate negative concepts or expound on depressing themes. However, I suspect that too often we deny the pain of our broken relationships or the disastrous events which happen in our lives. We hide our anger, our fears, and our frustrations; we put on a "brave, smiling face" to our world around us, and all that ever does is isolate us, thereby intensifying the pain, loneliness, and brokenness.

In *Man's Search For Meaning*, these words sum it up best:

> To live is to suffer, to survive is to find meaning in the suffering. If there is a purpose in life at all, there must be a purpose in suffering and in dying. But no man can tell another what this purpose is. Each must find out for himself, and must accept the responsibility that his answer prescribes. If he succeeds, he will continue to grow in spite of all "indignities."

Our unworld suffering must be faced and acknowledged—them we must deal with it if we are to *survive* and to *grow*.

Dr. Frankl is quite accurate when he writes and speaks

about the time when all is gone, everything seemingly is snatched away, and we are left with "the last of human freedoms." Then he describes that freedom as "the ability to choose one's attitude in a given set of circumstances."

I *choose* to accept God's forgiveness, His grace, and His mercy—*during* the unworld ordeal. I *choose* a positive and forgiving attitude. It may be the last of human freedoms, but a choice of attitude is definitely available. Color it HOPE.

Who Am I?

I asked, "Who am I?"

And the Lord answered quietly as a snowflake drifting down to embrace the land.

You are My child, My own, for whom I made the sun-drenched blue bonnets and the nestling down of a baby duck; the crisp smell of October's burning leaves; starry starry nights, and a Baby's birth-cry. You are My child, My little one that begs to crawl into her Daddy's lap and be rocked to sleep.

I asked, "Who am I?"

And Yahweh commanded the seas to roar and the winds to rave and the waves to pummel my tiny raft; to fling it high and crash it down; to dash salt-water over me, stinging my nakedness; to finally capsize my raft condemning me to drown in the icy dark water.

And as I founder, a strong hand grasps my shoulder, a hand that has always been there, and lifts me out to set me firmly on a new boat. You are My Beloved from whom I will never depart.

I cried, "Who am I?"

And God whirled round me with soldiers and swords, famine and locusts, riots and stones. Fools surrounded me and kings imprisoned me. Lightning flashed and volcanoes spewed. And through it all a hungering dark tugged my soul towards its jagged jaw. Deep within the howling I heard a shout: I am Creator, the Maker Omnipotent. You are My creation, My possession, My clay!

I sobbed, "Who am I?"

Tears fell on me as the Father kissed me. You are My Sparrow whom I have called by name. You are My Precious One for whom I weep, when you weep, and hunger when you hunger. You are My blessed Hope, My Joy for whom I would do anything, give anything so that

you might dance in My eternal kingdom.
You are my redeemed.

"Who am I?" I whispered.

You are a unique spirit, fashioned by hand in the image of Myself,
wrapped with the essence of Treasures and Gifts, quickened by Life-
Winds, awakened by Light.
You are who you are. Only that, and I love you.

—Beth Huffman Sikes

4

My own unplanned, unsystematic, and unexpected birth into the unworld experience came not in a brilliant flash of cognity; but slowly, almost lazily, it surfaced into focus. At a snail's pace with only an imperceptible amount of movement, the events unfolded and I had to accept, finally, the baptism of fire into the birth canal of the unworld ordeal. It was a most laborious and bewildering awakening. I was stunned and shocked by the reality.

I had spent years of my life, at least thirty or more, wearing thick blinders over my emotional heart and my conscious mind in my personal life. So much so that my denial of what was real in my life was as a solid wall around me which only reached new heights each year of living. In my defense, I can only say I did not deliberately lay out the bricks for the wall of denial, but neither did I believe I had any other choices.

When I look back at my life, I wish I could have known the lessons of the past few years back when I was a teenager or a twenty-year-old bride. I wish I'd listened to the voices of my parents or my own inner spirit. I wish I'd seen the tiny red warning flags waving from God's Spirit to mine . . . but I didn't. When I was fifteen or sixteen, I planned a very deliberate life strategy, as I wrote in *His Stubborn Love*.

1. I would be good, sweet, and charming at all costs. (Play-acting and masks would be the order of the day.)

2. I would go to church. (Especially when they asked me to sing.)
3. I would be kind and sweet to my parents and older people. (It generally paid off.)
4. I would attend and join various Christian youth activities. (Basing my choice on such important matters as who was in the group, what boys belonged, and where my music would be a stepping-stone.)
5. I would remember in the depths of my inner heart exactly what phonies Christians really were, and I would live my life as I saw fit. (In effect, I ordered, "God, You stay up there and I'll stay down here. You leave me alone, and I'll not bother You, and we'll *both* be happier.")

Then, I realize now, whatever was too painful, too destructive, or filled my young heart with too much suffering, I compromised; I made the necessary adjustments, arrangements, and choices to go on with life. Later, I said of my pending marriage and over the objections of my parents, "But, Mother, we *love* each other!" After marriage, I said I'd be strong. I'd go on and do what I felt, before God, I should do. I'd save myself as best I could from drowning in the sea of unworld despair.

It was as if I knew pain and suffering existed, but somehow I would try and deny its entry into my personal world. I began to view my life not as it really was, but as I wanted, dreamed, and hoped it would be.

I deliberately chose the attitudes I would have in life. Some were excellent choices, some left everything to be desired; still others were *dead* wrong.

When a situation called for change—I changed. When forgiveness was needed—I asked. When sacrifices were expected, I gave. When others had needs, I put aside my own. I'm well aware that these words can sound very self-serving, but they are true ... I did what countless other men and women have done ... I felt I had to be a super person. In my case, I had to be superwife, supermother, supergrandmother, and superwoman. The feeling persisted within me that if I could achieve this even seventy-five percent of the time, I would somehow escape personal suffering or at least keep it at arm's length for as long as I could.

I'm not sure what possessed me to keep a journal, off and on after I was married, or even why I kept hundreds of little written-on scraps of paper stuffed into notebooks, but I did. Writing letters all during my life is something I started when I was about sixteen, but at no time did I ever aspire to be a professional writer ... only a professional musician. In the 1950s, even though Al Sanders or Floyd Thatcher had not yet asked for me to write magazine articles or book-length manuscripts, I still managed to write some of my feelings down.

In 1959, when I was an active homemaker, wife, mother of two children, and very involved in my new life as a committed Christian dedicated to God, family, church, and community, I jotted down some thoughts in my journal about my day. I recall, of that day, that I had transplanted a whole tray of newly grown zinnia plants into the front porch planters. The small five- or six-inch tall plants had been taken from the tray, one by one, mudded-down-in, spaced well apart, and the soil was thoroughly watered.

The contrast in the way the plants looked, before and after I'd taken them out of their old soil and put them into the planters, was really pathetic. While they had been in their bedding tray, they stood up all tall and healthy looking. But now, poor dears, their stems and leaves were all drooping over and looking decidedly wilted. I told them that I understood their feelings of despair; but that soon, after they adjusted to their new home, they would be all right. I assured them they were only suffering temporarily from shock, that it was not painful; and soon, I promised, they would be all tall again and turn into beautiful bloomers.

Later that night, thinking of those zinnia plants in the front porch planters, I rather pompously wrote of transplantings: "There is no pain in being transplanted, either for zinnias or for people—only loneliness."

Oh, dear, could I have ever been that naive or that authoritative in my thinking? Obviously, I was. As you probably know, my statement about "no pain" was off about a billion light years. How pedantic those thoughts sound now. But what did I know then, at the age of twenty-seven, about transplantings—much less the complicated dichotomies of our lives, our relationships, and our world in general?

Time and reality, however, teach their own lessons. For I now know and understand that there is *both* pain *and* loneliness in being transplanted. Our ever-changing journey is an unbelievable one, which always seems to bring not only pain and loneliness, but a conglomerate of agonizing emotions as well.

What's more, I tended to carry the emotional hurts, the loneliness, and a deeply rooted inferiority complex—which were most painful to me—in a cast iron trunk over the most fragile bridges of my heart. I guess I felt it was easier to haul my hurts around, denying and repressing their existence, than it was to admit they were there and then have the problem of *dealing* with them. If you were like me, you simply would have found it easier to deny, to close your eyes to the unreconcilable relationships, the unexpected or unbearable physical or verbal abuse, the unkind responses of others towards yourself, and their neglect or avoidance of you.

Even now, when I look back on the past few years and view an unwise choice I made or see a glaring mistake, it still *seems* easier to carry the pain rather than admit it, examine it, and then *do* something about it. However, what I've come to understand about "keeping walls of denial" is that, most of the time, the cost of such thinking is too expensive and will often bankrupt our souls.

Of course, hindsight is an ever-ready resource. I only wish it were as easily accessible. I can now clearly see the obvious discrepancies between life as I would have liked it to have been and life as it really was!

The 1960s brought the first decade of unworld situations for me and my family, although I did not think of calling them by that name. In what seemed no time at all, after I wrote of "no pain, only loneliness," I had firsthand experience with the shocking effects of "transplantings." Any loneliness I might have encountered was, in those years, eclipsed by the searing, blinding fire of emotional pain. It was as if the roots of my life were roughly pulled and torn up by the death of my infant son, David. To have him die from the RH blood factor disorder (and to miss the simple cure, discovered shortly after), was—to my thinking—*unfair* and *unfathomable!* To have him cremated instead of buried to save us money, since hospital costs were high was—to my heart's reasoning—*unforgivable,* but I crept behind the walls of my denial.

Not only were my roots pulled from the soil of my soul, but exactly one year to the day of David's funeral, my darling Grandpa Uzon died. A few days later, as his family's funeral procession pulled up to the grave site, my mother was too ill from the chemotherapy—used to treat her breast cancer—to get out of the mortuary limousine . . . so I sat with her; and, together, we mourned the passing of Papa—her father, my grandfather.

I begged the Lord that day to somehow replant my torn roots, to do no more pruning, no more severing of beloved ties, no more losses. At least, would He grant me a break . . . for now? I reasoned that if there were some interval of time, some respite from the pruning, or at least a breathing spell for a little while—then maybe, just maybe, we could all gain back some energy, even store a little in reserve, and grow again . . . possibly, I'd bloom a bit. I didn't understand, back then, the positive effects that suffering can bring in one's character. Nor did I know of the growth of inner strength that incredibly horrible times can forge.

However, on the day of Grandpa's funeral, each time I noted the greyness of my mother's once clear olive skin, saw the fatigue of death about her shoulders, and searched in vain for the sparkle which had always glittered in her dark brown eyes— I sensed there would be no let up, no hiatus of pruning. I struggled with the ever-burgeoning concept of *more* losses, *more* grief, and *more* pain. I felt this whole matter of living and dying was so unfair and so wrong . . . at the same time, I knew both life and death were unescapable.

True to my foreboding thoughts, it was only nine months later that I watched as cancer ate away the vivacious life of my fifty-seven-year-old mother.

During the mid-sixties, I took a good look at my life, or my garden, if you will. My baby son, my grandfather, and my dearest friend, my mother, were all gone. Pruned out of my life. I took no comfort from the fact that I'd see them in heaven one day . . . I wanted to see them here and now! In the black well of pain and grief which followed, I did not believe I'd live through it nor did I even care to. My views of God portrayed Him as the master gardener who, with no apparent concern over my suffering, had decided, almost capriciously, that He would not only prune this rose bush, but that He would work large amounts of fertilizer into the soil around me . . . burning and stinging what was left of my tender, exposed roots.

It is possible that you've never lost a very close loved one, and so it's difficult for you to conceive how grief could be this overwhelming. Or maybe you have lost far more than I, and you've tasted infinitely greater amounts of devastating sorrow. Maybe, like Viktor Frankl, you have lived through the horror of a concentration camp; or, maybe you opened the garage door to be the first one to see the lifeless body of your seventeen-year-old son hanging from the ceiling beams. All I really know is that pain is pain . . . suffering is suffering . . . and grief is grief. As Dr. Frankl pointed out: the suffering of our lives fills up each and every space within us, whether the space is big or small. It still hurts to suffer.

By the time I reached the middle seventies, I was involved in a writing career and had several published books which, on their own, became a journalizing of my life's events. Even in my denial of life as it really was, I was beginning to formulate a name for the dichotomy of pain and pleasure, of sorrow and joy; and was concluding . . . then as now . . . that we all live on a planet which is not called Earth, but a planet named *Unworld.*

Around that time, early into the beginning stages of my acceptance in believing that the earth was really the unworld—and yet hardly anticipating anything about the unworld trials yet to come to me—I wrote, in a Sunday School *Power For Living* column of mine, this prayer:

Dear Lord,

There are the people, children, and I who seem so *unteachable;*

there are the stresses of daily life which at times are *unbelievable;*

the marriages which, unless You work a miracle, are *unreconcilable;*

the continuing stabs of pain which are *unbearable;*

the unwanted feelings about others which are *unprintable;*

the events of tomorrow which are *unpredictable;*

the mountains before me which are *unmovable;*

the deaths of small children which are *unfathomable*;

the attitudes of others, and myself, which are *unreasonable*;

the sins I committed today which are *unconscionable*;

the goals I set for tomorrow which are *unobtainable*;

the visions and dreams which are all *unfulfilled*;

the closed doors which make me feel *unwanted*;

the traffic citations which are *unjustified*;

the crisis which is *unexpected* and *unbidden*;

And the list goes on.

So thank You, Lord

that Your love is *unlimited*;

Your grace *unending*;

Your mercy *unshakable*;

Your forgiveness *undeserved*;

and the chain of blessings in my life *unbroken*.

In the following decade, I was to experience firsthand each and every unworld example in that prayer. It is still unthinkable to me that these brief words could so accurately predict my future circumstances.

While I didn't lose any more close and dearly loved family members to the grave during the seventies, I was in no way prepared for the unexpected events which were about to happen in my journey. For suddenly, even though I was walking close to our Lord, a new terror took over. Almost instantly, I went into the familiar patterns of denial and I was frozen with shock. Two questions pushed past my desire to deny: one was, What in the world is God doing? And, secondly, How in the world am I to react and respond?

The unworld catastrophe which seemed to come out of nowhere, striking me with the immense force of a tornado, was pain. The unexpected and terrible world of pure *physical pain.*

Its official name was Temporalmandibular Joint Stress Dysfunction (TMJ, for short). I was consumed by pain involving the jaw joint, the muscles around it, my teeth, my sinuses, my eyes, my ears, my entire head, and my shoulder muscles. After a few months, the pain intensified; and when it would reach "level four," there was both diarrhea and vomiting. In the beginning, TMJ pain occurred on an occasional basis, but in a little less than three years—after dentists and doctors had been seen, and therapy had been done—the pain became chronic, settling in on almost an everyday basis. I tracked the levels of pain on my calendar; over and over again, it would show 20 to 30 days of unworld physical pain each month.

I kept the pain hidden as best I could from my family and my co-workers and friends. I would have never gone public with it, in any way, except that I was having to cancel speaking engagements and I was losing vast amounts of writing time to the blinding pain. Finally, I was forced to give an explanation for cutting down the schedule; so, in a book called *The High Cost of Growing,** I dealt with the new phenomenon: physical suffering. I did not dream that thousands of persons would respond to me, nor did I foresee how meaningful writing about an illness would be in helping others. Yet, sharing the ordeal of TMJ pain was—and still is, to this day—continuing to bring a measure of healing. I am not saying that I am—as some faith healers do—"claiming" healings, but I know the truth that often God uses suffering of one individual for His own special healing in the life of someone else. I'm not sure why it works; only that it does.

There is no need to rehash the ten-year battle with the

The High Cost of Growing, by Joyce Landorf. Copyright © 1978. Published by Thomas Nelson Publishers.

pain and stress of TMJ—nor of all the emotional damage and, equally as destructive, the side effects in the life and family of anyone who suffers with a chronic pain problem. But for those of you whose unworld crisis is a matter of daily physical pain, here are some feelings from a pain journal which I wrote of in my book *Silent September*.

Naively I always think that pain can do *nothing more* to me. Yet I am always wrong.

There is a certain amount of head knowledge within me that says someday the Lord, in His mercy, will step in and stop this hideous round of pain, which is attacking on a never-ending basis. Isn't that what a loving heavenly Father would do? Yet here, in my heart, I cannot see, hear, touch, or feel God; and the silence of my life is deadly. God seems to be doing nothing—at all.

Continually I rationalize that after pain has robbed, raped, and smashed the courage and hope out of me, it will have spent its fury—like the last gusts of wind from a retreating thunderstorm. Often I fantasize that since pain has devoured so much of me already, my dues into the I've-suffered-enough-account have been paid in full, and there will be no need for further payment. Or, I think, at least pain will lessen the force of its rage and give me *some* respite from its devastation.

But, it seems I tend to underestimate the enormous penetrating power of pain. I minimize the tenacity of its excruciating grip. Somehow I hold tightly to the crumb of hope which says *maybe*, just maybe, I'll be mysteriously and miraculously given the grace and strength of God to go on, in spite of these crushing encounters.

Yet, with each new day, pain swoops down like a huge demolition crane, swinging and smashing its steel and concrete ball of destruction against the flimsy walls of my battered body and soul. I'm left shattered, broken, and without a shred of hope.

I am no novice in walking the paths of pain. And I am no stranger to climbing the mountains of grief suffering. But this—this, I do *not* understand, for suddenly I am aware that I don't hear the music anymore.

I'm a nightingale with broken wings. I'm a nightingale without a song. Oh yes, it's true that I'm a born "night-singer"—one who can sing the sweetest songs of God, even in the darkest dead of night. But now, now I don't hear the music of God or His angels and I am frightened . . . alone . . . and hurting unbearably. . . .

I am also angry! And not just for me, but for millions of others. This is unfair. It's unjust. It's undeserved! . . .

I don't know where to turn for help anymore. The darkness is too deep, and the God-silence is too great. I am isolated, lonely, untouchable. Worst of all, because I can't hear the music of God anymore, I feel like an abandoned orphan. Maybe someday someone will come along and rescue me, adopt me, and hold me in their arms of love until the pain subsides. But who? I've sung and written the music of God for thousands of others. Won't anyone now sing for me? Won't anyone bind up what pain has broken and help me hear the music once more?

I pray that you who are suffering from the debilitating effects and stresses of physical pain will in some way know that, because of my very silent Septembers, I *do* know you are special. And we who hurt—hurt *with* you, and we *do* understand and we care.

As to my journey, it seemed to me that as the griefs and losses of the 1950s merged with the intensification of physical pain in the 1970s, I felt something—somewhere inside my mind or body—was going to have to break apart, snapping in two like some dry, brittle twig. That feeling persisted and surged so much that by the 1980s . . . a little more than twenty years after I started that first journal with my simplistic and rather shallow comments on transplanting zinnias . . . I was now writing about the dreaded sense of endings, of finality, and of termination. I could foresee no future for myself, so there was nothing to aim for, nothing that would keep my heart and soul here on earth. No reason to continue and no "why" for living. Who but my private journal could I tell? Who would believe me? I thought most people would say, "Are you kidding? You're a superstar author. You're on the National Religious Best Seller book list. You have more reason to live than anyone . . . you're a success!"

But because pain from my jaw joint dysfunction left me with precious little mental, emotional, or physical energy and was continually wasting the small amounts of strength I still possessed, my foreboding persisted. My thoughts and reasoning grew darker in the early 1980s and I had to face the truth that, more often than not, I was in a state of despair . . . not merely a semi-bad feeling, but genuine despair. My denial wall was being demolished by the hammers and pickaxes of reality. I had ever-increasing glimpses of truth and the pending disaster which would come with it, or the ending of my life—whichever would come first. Again, I never anticipated the terrible price I would pay for building the wall of denial in the first place.

Looking back, I know now that had I been free from the violent levels of pain, I would have written out a list of sorts, about my life—just as I had done during other stressful times. On paper, I would have summed up the pros and cons of the times; and, in short, if I had done this, I could have taken stock of some of the major events and problem areas. I didn't write out that list because I was too ill . . . but, if I had written it out, it would have probably read something like this:

Those were the years that I—

- Worked inside and outside the home,
- Raised two children,
- Saw them married to fine, beautiful people,

- Held my first granddaughter, April Joy,
- Moved households several times,
- Decorated and furnished houses into homes,
- Put wallpaper and paint along with laughter into the walls,
- Sang and spoke for too-many-to-mention Mother and Daughter banquets each year,
- Broadcast a daily radio program for seven years,
- Saw both my brother, Cliff, and my sister, Marilyn, married to fine people and begin their families,
- Encouraged, supported my husband and children in their endeavors,
- Traveled and lectured all over the world,
- Shared seminars for several years with Dr. James Dobson,
- Recorded three vocal albums and many speaking tapes,
- Gave countless interviews for all kinds of media,
- Appeared on national and local radio and TV programs,
- Endured increasing amounts of chronic pain,
- Received a number of awards from various organizations,
- Underwent countless dental, medical, and psychological procedures
- Welcomed three more grandchildren—Ricky, James, and Jennifer,
- Learned much in pain control clinics,
- Suffered the exhaustion of stress (mentally, emotionally, and physically) caused by pain,
- Worked through to forgiveness with my Irregular person,
- Became a weekly Bible study teacher in the California desert
- Filmed six lectures for a film series, and, during those years,
- Wrote one book every ten months.

Even now, as I read this list back to myself, I don't think that anyone ever *plans* to be that over-involved, that active, or that busily occupied. It just evolves sometimes out of sheer necessity. Often, too, we are aware of the need to fill the voids of our own or others in family relationships so we go at it with all our strength. It has been said that the wise person is one who can pace herself through life. But I have found that often the ability to pace and schedule one's time is a solid-gold luxury, which is more available to us in the last years of our lives and comes at a time when we don't really want it or need it. I seemed to have no special talent for getting things done, only large amounts of drive and energy.

My life the past thirty years was never boring, but then any woman knows the truth of that if she has managed a home, a family, and has also taken on adult schooling, work, career, or a profession. There is always another task, a duty, a meeting, or a project to tackle. My attitude of denial about hurtful things allowed me to enjoy the whole procedure, especially *before* the incredible pain took over; so I invested much love, time, prayer, talent, and energy in the effort to take care of everybody and everything.

I am still surprised at how much was accomplished, although I never did get around to cleaning out the refrigerator properly, nor did I ever paint or wallpaper with as much precision as was called for; and certainly I never learned how to look extremely interested during discussions about the weather or other small talk at neighborhood coffee klatches or dinner parties.

If you have read any of my books, you know that I have tried to reveal life and relationships as openly and candidly as possible. I need to tell you that I wrote the truth about my life. I did not, knowingly, deceive anyone. My works, with the exception of two biblical novels, were nonfiction and autobiographical in nature . . . and I did not make up or even exaggerate the stories I told about my family, myself, my personal life, or marriage.

However, I *did* do two things which rocked and lulled me into a false sense of security and which built the walls of my denial a little higher around me. (Those walls protected my mind and soul from seeing the world around me as it really was.) First . . . in tapes or books or on speaking tours, I told mostly about the good, the bright, the victorious, and the lovely events of my life. If I wanted to use an illustration that might have put someone in my family in a bad light, even temporarily, I cleared each and every sentence and paragraph with the family member I was quoting. I read them the whole illustration or example and, in every instance, they agreed that what I had written was true. Wholeheartedly, they gave me the permission to use the material as I saw fit. So I did not use anything without my husband's or my children's consent, and I did not intentionally share the darker inner sides of my life. Carefully, I drew a curtain around those events of my life and my responses to them, especially when they were too painful for me to handle.

I did not discuss the strains or the pressures which came with being a highly visible public person. I did not share or confide to anyone the mental and emotional anxieties I was suffering in my marriage, or of the relationships at home that were severely impaired, gravely wounded or, worse, dead. I never felt I had the right to expose my own personal struggles or those of anyone in my family. I kept my private anguish out of my public life, books, and speaking engagements as carefully as I could. I simply did not reveal the marital conflicts, my persistent loneliness, or the intimate depths of my despair which had become a basic part of my heart and soul.

In my mind, it was my burden and mine alone. It was also too painful to explain; and, besides that, I thought my public and my peers wanted the image of an untarnished-saint-on-a-pedestal to be the visible part of my life, so I kept my hurts locked up and just between God and me. I also kept those dark issues from my children, my family, my pastor, and even my closest friends.

Last week I met a woman at one of my speaking engagements who talked briefly with me about her own marriage, separation, and unworld experience. Today, I received a warm, encouraging letter from her. However, she was struggling with my book, *Tough And Tender*, because she felt the book led people to believe that I had all the answers, trappings, and makings of a "happy, even scriptural marriage." Then she added, "The book is so good, but is it a fraud?"

That's a valid question, but it should be pointed out that I wrote several books about my marriage—including the one the woman was reading—*before* the onset of TMJ. Pain had not yet begun to do its immense physical and emotional damage in my personal life.

Secondly, as I said, I have not told the dark specific details of the painful disintegration of my marriage relationship. How could I have written those crushing details if I couldn't admit, even to myself, that they existed? In my own life, I denied there was any breaking down of communications, any subtle or obvious emotional abuses, any deep needs or voids unfilled, or any lack of understanding, neglect, or the absence of knowledge about one's personhood. I have the feeling that, out of respect for human dignity, anyone would have chosen to do the same thing and kept it a private matter of the heart and soul.

It is interesting to note that the woman, in writing me, listed several very dark details describing the marital strife in her own marriage. I feel certain that, even though she was safe and free to tell me, it would be unthinkable for her to go to her church or Sunday School class and share the same dark, private areas of her life in a public way.

It is only fair to say that a few—very few—of my family

and friends *were* discerning and perceptive. In rather hushed and quiet tones, and sometimes without words, they let me know that they saw the emotional pain and stress in me. Somehow, they assured me of their understanding hearts on my behalf. They were a rare, wonderful minority who, without knowing *any* details, told me they would be on my side, in my "balcony"; and they prayed for my wholeness. They did me a great favor—they took me off a preconceived and phony pedestal and did not demand perfection from me, but allowed me to be as human as they were.

One such person, a minister and author, looked directly at me, took my hand—after I'd spoken to several thousand people at Praise Gathering in Indianapolis—and said (as nearly as I can recall), "Joyce, I am committing, here and now, to pray daily for you ... I can sense you are really hurting. ..." I looked up at him, expecting to hear that his prayers would be about my jaw and physical pain, for I had just spoken on *Silent September*, but he finished his brief remarks to me with: "You're hurting at home, aren't you?" I could only weep and nod yes. Gently, he finished, "Don't say anything. I don't need any details. I know it's at home, so just know I'll be praying."

One wrote and said, "I have no idea why I feel so burdened to keep you in my prayers—but almost every day, your name goes through my mind."

Another young woman summed it up when she said, "I don't know what all you've been through, Joyce, but whatever it is, or was, it must have dragged you through barbed wire fences."

Keeping the dark sides of my life hidden wasn't the only way I attempted to cope with the insurmountable and multiplying private agonies which began in dreadful ways in the 1980s. In an effort to try to be the person God wanted me to be, I *idealized* my personal life, my marriage, and my relationships into what I longed, hoped, and preferred to see . . . not what they actually were.

Admitting to anyone that the complicated hurts of my marital state were real was almost impossible for me to do as a Christian leader. Also, speaking or writing about the dark side of marriage seemed to be more painful than keeping on the blinders of my denial. So I endured, very much alone and very desperate; while, at the same time, I was astounded to discover that almost everything the Lord chose to do through me became extremely successful. I was as surprised at the success, the acclaim, and the high visibility and the superstar pedestals that go with success as I was with the sadness and misery that continually clipped the wings of my inner soul.

As every public person knows, the dichotomy between public success and acclaim and a personal sense of loneliness and failure is enormous. I tried to keep the dark issues hidden. I did not want to hurt my family or suggest the outrageous possibility that suffering might *very well* be connected to them or a genuine part of God's plan. And, at the time, I didn't have the faintest idea of how desperately I would wish to die in order to escape from physical and emotional pain. It was easier to keep it all bottled up inside.

I did what I believe most Christian women wearing my shoes would have done. For it is true that almost from the onset of our walk with God, we are programmed like some innate computer to put on a happy face, to smile, to be victorious, to be cheerful, and to appear upbeat. We are to share only the positive, happy-ending stories. It's as if someone wrote a scenario that has these basic points:

1. How bad I used to be—
2. Then I found God.
3. How good I am now—

4. How wonderful, how peaceful, how fantastic, how perfect is my future.
5. I can endure *anything* until I get to heaven.

We are taught to ignore, or at least downplay, anything from the more unpleasant ordeals to the worst of scenarios. This teaching is prevalent and works fine, right up until the moment when an unworld horror levels all our walls and pulls away our masks. Then, because we think others around us are beautiful, picture-perfect people, and because we don't know that their mask is firmly in place just like ours, we think we are isolated and completely alone in this tragedy.

We feel there is no one in our family, our church, our neighborhood, or our world who will understand. And sure enough, if we *do* scrape up the courage to tell our pastor, family, friends, or someone in our church or community . . . we can almost count on it . . . that person is unwilling or unable to face their own inadequacies and hurts, so they are *"appalled"* at what we reveal with our honesty. Our truthfulness blows them away, and they back away from us with incredible speed. It's only natural that we end up being very sorry we shared any personal circumstances, and we are left feeling stupid and way out of line. We see that the fabricated victorious life of a Christian does not begin to match up to the reality of the unworld life we really do live.

So, it's safer to cover up our humiliations, hurts, and anxieties. And, it's much safer to be quiet than to talk.

Little do we realize that the person sitting next to us in church, on a bus, at our place of work, or in a grocery store is wearing a carefully placed joy mask to hide their contorted, pain-lined face, and that they are feeling like there is no one in the world who understands or cares. This is especially true for pastors and people in positions of Christian leadership, for if we admit we are experiencing some kind of unworld trauma, we appear to be doubting God's ability to solve problems; or it seems we are ungrateful to God for past intervention, and maybe even a little embarrassed by God's "apparent" lack of concern. As our friend, Mike Cloer, wrote,

> We are teaching a wholesale Christianity that would imply a rose with no thorns by simply turning everything over to God. Much like a man is programmed to hide his pain (or not to cry) because to do otherwise would appear unmanly. . . .
>
> As Christians, we feel we have to conceal our questions, doubts, and pains so as not to give the impression of aspersing Christ. To do so would take away some of our firepower in converting the unbeliever. . . .
>
> For some unknown reason, when a Christian falls down, he quickly jumps up, looks around to see if anyone has seen (and, if so, even hurt, he will go out of his way to assure us that he is okay with no injury), and then he'll remark, in some fashion, as to how dumb it was to have fallen. We Christians have been doing that, and then forging ahead without looking back or investigating as to why we tripped in the first place.

Eventually, the dark sides of my life—the darker thoughts of suicide, and the black despair—gathered together privately and silently like hot, molten lava and finally exploded over the sides of my unworld volcano . . . they refused to stay underneath the surface of my conscious mind and I came face to face with the fiery holocaust within me.

I truly believed that nothing, absolutely nothing, could happen to me that would be worse than the years of daily high-intensity TMJ pain. Doctors, dentists, or my own research could never find a pain medication or drug which had any effect on the pain. My only relief came a few times a year when I was given an injection of Demerol to break the pain cycle; then, mercifully, I was granted sleep for two or three days.

I was also completely convinced that there was no trauma—physical, mental, or emotional—which could wipe out my life, my creativity, and my energy the way physical pain did. I felt nothing more deplorable or degrading or unspeakable could ever touch me or happen in view of what I'd already endured.

Some people are born into their frightening unworld experience in one all-shattering instant—during an unexpected phone call, possibly during an unforeseen conference with a doctor, or upon discovering unnerving evidence about someone. For others, they are pressed unsteadily into the unworld crisis overnight or over the course of hours, weeks, or maybe even months. With me, it took a fairly long time to admit the unworld volcano had indeed erupted. My layers of denial were thick; and, since the unworld experience is "what happens to others—not to me," I was certain *nothing* could be worse and the unthinkable would *not* happen to me!

That unthinkable thing, that unbelievable thing that could never happen to me was all wrapped up in one and only one word:

The word *DIVORCE.*

From the time of childhood, when my father was a minister, we did not have one person in our family who was divorced. I was not aware of knowing *anyone* who had divorced in our family until I was in my teens. Even from my engagement, at eighteen years of age, and during some thirty years of my own marriage which followed, never did I personally consider a separation, much less a divorce. In the fifth year of that marriage, I almost succeeded in taking my life; but even at that terrible time, divorce was *not* an option, not an alternative, and certainly not a choice. Suicide, yes . . . a distinct possibility—but not divorce.

To this day, the word *divorce* sticks in my throat, and my tongue finds it almost unpronounceable. In my big, forty-pound Webster dictionary, it shows the *"un-"* prefix to mean "not, lack of, the opposite of," such as the word *unhappy. Un* also is a prefix meaning "back" and is added to verbs such as *unlock.* Then, in this huge dictionary, there follows several pages of words with the "un" prefix—beginning with the word *unabased* and ending with *unzoned.* It's no small matter that there are six columns of words on each page, and each column has 103 words; roughly, there are over 2,500 *"un-* words"! I think most of them can be applied to the experience of having something happen which you *believed* could never happen to you. Like the word *divorce.*

While I was in the stage of denial, I was fond of quoting various Christian women leaders, like Dale Evans Rogers, who was a wonderful personal friend to my mother and still is to me; or Ruth Graham, whom I've never met, but love. I admired, and still do, these beautiful women; and I most heartily agreed with them when they were asked if they'd ever considered a divorce. Their answer ran something like this: "Consider divorce? No. That is not an option for me as a Christian woman." Then, humorously, they added, "Murder? Maybe. But not divorce."

Drilled into my Christian background was the sanctity of marriage, the seriousness of the marriage vows, and the oft-preached sermons on who or what qualified one for biblical divorce proceedings; but, most of all, I was taught the importance of keeping my own commitment to marriage. My mother and grandmother had stayed in their marriages with a deep sense of commitment, so it was a foregone conclusion . . . I would stay in mine.

But even when I sensed the vague stirrings of marital pressure and stress which seeped through my structured denial early in the 1970s, and I felt I needed some kind of direction, there was very little counseling or professional help available from Christian sources. Worse, there was virtually no place to go for a pastor or Christian leader when their own lives needed confidential counseling. It seemed that all leadership and lay leaders—including the music director, organists, deacons, board members, soloists, or Sunday School teachers—were *supposed* to have perfect marriages and perfect children. They were to also have perfectly wonderful relationships worked out with everyone. And as long as the bad parts or the painful parts of their lives remained sealed from public view, then they were still usable. So those of us in Christian leadership did the best we could and carried on, not because we had perfect marriages and families, but rather because it was *expected* of us. Carrying on and moving ahead was also expected of God. The theory was that we were to carry on with our public ministry, *no matter what the circumstances of our personal lives were,* and God would do the same, taking care of everything and moving straight ahead.

On a typically beautiful fall day in 1983, by the Pacific Ocean in Del Mar, California, the brick walls of my denial and blatant refusal to see my life as it really was began to fall apart. I found it increasingly difficult to stay behind my happy mask or to hide my emotional scars or present wounds. I found this out in rather ordinary ways, after begging God to stop the physical pain.

One day I realized I had not had a comprehensive physical checkup in several years. Taking the time to get a physical exam was complicated because I was totally and completely strung out emotionally, mentally, physically, and even spiritually, by the grinding process of TMJ pain. There were hardly one or two days a month when I experienced *any* lowering of pain levels. Also, by now, the pain broke its usual "days only" pattern of ending around 11:00 P.M., as it had been doing, and now came back about 2:00 or 3:00 in the morning, to begin the cycle all over again.

When I thought about having a physical exam, I hardly

knew where to start, and I was so exhausted that I hoped someone would come up with a good idea. Fortunately, a new family doctor recommended the Executive's Physical Fitness program at Scripps Memorial Hospital in La Jolla. So an appointment was made, cancelled once because of too much pain, and then finally made again; and, over several days, the examination took place. I was checked and tested by the various specialists and found that they were a very dedicated and exceptional group of doctors. My examinations were thorough and complete.

At one point, immediately after I had been tested on the treadmill, the cardiologist in charge said, "Mrs. Landorf, there is nothing intrinsically wrong with your heart—but," he went on quite matter-of-factly, "you are going to be dead within a year, either by some disease or by your own hand, unless you lower the stress levels of your life." He then ordered written stress evaluations and tests to be taken in order to determine the basic root problem. He, and several other doctors, felt that if I could lower the stress levels, I'd probably experience a general lowering of TMJ pain. It was the first ray of hope for me regarding physical pain. And just the idea that *maybe* the pain would not reach such high intensities was an incredibly thrilling thought. However, the doctor's warning to me about the damage stress was doing, internally and mentally, to my system knocked the top several rows of brick clean off my denial wall. I knew I was going to have to face the most painful experiences of my life—and this time I would *have* to deal with them.

I have repressed much of the conversation that day with the doctors who gave and evaluated my physical and written tests. Again, it was easier to fall back into an old pattern and repress that which was too painful.

What I do remember vividly is that one of the written stress tests had thirty or forty questions, and the answers were to be checked into two columns. One check indicated that yes, the event described had happened, and the other column was for the count of how many times this particular event happened during this year. (For instance: "Have you moved your home in the past year? If yes, then how many times?" A high stress score of 300 points was very bad and indicated you had an eighty percent chance of coming down with some major illness within the year. The procedure followed was that after the doctors evaluated all the test answers, then they would help the patient work out plans for lowering his or her stress levels.

My score on that particular test was not a high 300. It was 721. It is interesting to me now to recall that before the doctors had finished with their evaluation of all the tests, in my case, most of them told me they felt that the enormously high levels of stress were probably caused by my work. My speaking/traveling, writing/broadcasting, etc. Their first, off-the-cuff suggestions were that I should completely stop all activities—writing and speaking specifically—for three to six months' rest.

Accepting those early speculations was easy for me because it allowed me to stay a few more days behind my denial wall. In the meantime, one of the doctors expressed interest in my being an author. So I gave him a few books and one video, "Changepoints," from the film series, *His Stubborn Love.*

A week or so later, I was asked to come in to the hospital for a brief preliminary meeting to evaluate some of the tests.

Immediately, the doctors started off the discussion by explaining that they had to revise a previously stated opinion. It seems they had spoken too soon and had not properly identified the source of my high stress levels. One doctor further noted that they did not feel that the unmanageable stress in my life was brought about by my speaking, traveling, and intensive writing schedule. Then, warmly, he went on for a moment or two about my books and films. In fact, all the doctors and physical therapists were very affirmative, and enthusiastically encouraged me to continue my work—which one doctor called "Your incredible gift!" ending with, "You must *not* stop your work!"

As they were talking about my writing and speaking, I began to feel slightly uneasy and unsettled. Mentally, I began pulling out of the room, long before I did so physically; and, even though the conference room was comfortably warm, I was suddenly chilled to the bone. I found myself not wanting to hear their conclusion.

It didn't take too much reasoning to understand that if my work, career, calling, or whatever you wanted to name it, was *not* responsible for the high levels of stress in my life, then it had to be *something* else. Or perhaps, *someone* else. . . . Abruptly I got up out of my chair. There was no way I could stay there and face that kind of implication or listen to the logic of their findings.

The quiet words of one doctor stopped me at the door— "When you are ready to listen to our evaluations and recommendations—come back in. We'll be here."

Three weeks later, I received the culmination of all the staff reports on my test results in the mail, and I was requested to make an appointment for a conference to discuss their evaluations and suggestions.

Now very disturbed and apprehensive, I went back to the hospital conference room. My worst fearful suspicions came true. The stress levels were *not* primarily associated with my heavy work schedule, but closely identified with an individual. As the doctors went over my written stress tests and laid out the truth before me, I could no longer close my eyes to my life or marriage as it was, nor could I idealize it into what I wanted it to be. Clearly, it was understood that I would have to deal with the inescapable truths of the long-standing, emotionally destructive patterns in my marriage, of my deep loneliness, of my general despair.

I was pleased to find that while my jaw pain was caused by TMJ, it was not psychosomatic or psychogenic in origin. Stress triggered the daily pain sequence, aggravated it, and extended both the length and the duration of suffering. My body was most definitely telling me, in no uncertain terms, that it could no longer accept any more additional negative emotional stress. My jaw and head were screaming their message to me, and I could hardly ignore them. Now the doctors were saying that it was my responsibility to lower the stress levels and to do it quickly. I had to listen and pay attention to what was being said. Mostly, I knew I was going to have to deal with the basic root problem. It would no longer be possible for me to bury myself in writing another book or involving myself in more work, as I'd always done, or to lie to myself and say everything was all right.

The concept of our body's ability to give us a message through physical pain, and of the unthinkable conflict within us, was not entirely new to me.

For a number of years my friend and gynecologist, Dr. Jitu Bhatt, had stressed the importance of listening to what our bodies tell us. He understood the value of this so well that he encouraged not only me, but all his patients, to hear with their inner ear the message that was trying to surface. His strongest and most direct conversation about the high levels of pain and the connection between physical pain and emotional conflict came the day after my hysterectomy surgery. I heard him clearly; but, even then, I crept away from the sound of his voice and hid behind my denial walls.

However, during my recovery time, my friend, Keith Miller, phoned one day; and he addressed the same issue as Dr. Bhatt. He stressed the need for us to recognize our body's ability to give us important messages. Then, in a long and detailed letter, Keith followed up on the call.

Keith had personally known Dr. Paul Tournier and had studied the works of this great psychiatrist. Keith had also experienced his own unworld ordeals. Here are some excerpts from his warm and candid letter.

... Dr. Tournier indicated that all illness has a meaning for the life of the one who is ill. He does not say that God sends illness as a telegram. But he says that in one sense, the unconscious does. In other words, if there is something up within us which is too frightening or upsetting to face consciously, but which would threaten our image of ourself or our conscious values, then we repress that knowledge from our conscious mind. But the way we are made, according to Tournier, we cannot long tolerate the inner separation this unfaced conflict causes. The unconscious has no "voice" except through the body and dreams. (Both of which are used by the unconscious a little like we use charades to try to get a title or idea across to our team in the game, "Charades.") So that we do not get a direct understandable message from our tearful and agonized unconscious (heart). But we experience symptoms of illness and pain. This illness or pain is like a telegram in a foreign language from our deepest, buried self crying in even louder tones, "Listen to me!" The conflict within you is so dangerous that *you must hear* this message and change your behavior or direction or the deepest part of you will surely die.

As the message gets louder, the pain gets more serious until one uncovers the message, or the part of the body where the pain is focused breaks down. This may be why normally curable things are stubborn to treatment. . . .

This of course is only a theory. And it is not saying that *God* is *sending* pain. It is saying that God has designed our personalities so that they will not tolerate inner dissonance without trying to get us to face and deal with our very deepest needs and conflicting desires.

Over the years, I have begun to face one deep inner conflict after another. And I discovered some shattering things about myself and my needs . . . which I had never really faced consciously. I'd evidently been afraid at a very deep (unconscious) level that if I faced and voiced some of my most basic feelings about my life and my needs, for instance, that people wouldn't deal with them and would reject me. And yet when, through Tournier, my needs and feelings became *conscious*, I had to deal with them.

To find the meaning of an illness—*whatever the physical cause*—this process of Tournier's has changed my life. And *if* this is a true approach (and it is only one man's theory and I have been *very simplistic* in presenting Tournier's thirty books in a few pages), but if this approach is true, then trying to figure out "why God doesn't stop the pain" *could* be dealing with the wrong question.

But I know that, as paradoxical as it seems, I believe that God has set in motion a marvelous system by which in our freedom we can never wander too far away from the needs and desires and values (which may conflict with our *conscious* desires and values) which are in our bones, so to speak. Once we get our true desires and feelings out, we don't have to act on them if they are *not* in line with our present commitments. But as we *face* them, they can no longer "make me sick."*

Because of what Keith had written and what the doctors at Scripps Memorial Hospital had confirmed, I understood that if anything was to be done about the stress related parts of my pain, I would have to do it, and much of the work would have to be done within my marriage. But I wondered how I would survive *staying* in the marriage? I'd barely lived through the ordeal of chronic pain the previous ten years—how could I stay on? Or worse, how could I legally separate when, as a Christian, I was so *dead set* against separation and divorce? As Keith said, "Such a paradox!"

---

*For a discussion of the biblical roots of denial and its effects on God's people, see *Sin: Overcoming the Deadly Addiction*, by Keith Miller. Published by Harper and Row, Publishers, Inc. Copyright © 1987.

The hellacious crisis which scorched my heart and mind that day was the blackest of my entire lifetime. I truly saw no choices, no options, no solutions, save one: to take my life and escape the unworld's dilemma and stranglehold. Never had I felt so damaged beyond repair. I began collecting pain pills so I would have enough to use at the appropriate time.

Some of the events the last half of 1983 are fresh and clear in my memory, but many of them are blurred with the over-all agony of those times. Just today, at this writing, I went back to my notebooks, journal books, and my heavily marked-up 1983 calendar. There was such a rush of emotions and such contrasts due to the mix of experiences and circumstances. Reading and reliving those events, especially the calendar, brought back all the feelings of those days as if they had happened last Tuesday. Grafted out before me I could see there were a few rare moments of joy, but very few. Occasionally there was some pride in a person, an event, or in a circumstance. Mostly, there was pain, and deep wells of sadness. Here are some of the highlights from my records:

- There was the well-orchestrated and well-planned start up of a national radio broadcast ... *From The Heart Of Joyce.* And for the first time, I had a nonprofit corporation and a board of directors.
- There was the organizing of the ministries' offices to handle the radio program, staffed by some very specially gifted people.
- There was a close-to-home yet secluded office (every writer dreams about!) for me to write and work in. The manuscript of *He Began With Eve* was being written at that time.
- There was sitting on a hospital bed with my daughter, Laurie, at the exact moment of my grandbaby, Jennifer's, birth. There was also the awesome feelings about the miracle I'd

just witnessed and the overwhelming feeling of love and pride for Laurie and my son-in-law, Terry.

- There was major surgery, a hysterectomy, the last month of 1983. The aloneness of seclusion and bed rest at home, seeing very few family members or friends, gave me a brief six weeks' respite from the intensive TMJ pain. It also lent a credibility to the Scripps doctors' theories about the pressures of stress and my own ability to lower it.

But it was still too difficult for me to believe my body's messages, my doctors' findings, my friends' evaluations, or my own inner soul's pleading. So, nothing changed with the coming of 1984 except that there were more pressures than ever, and the internal stress and physical pain had increased on all sides.

A counselor friend advised us to obtain some concentrated professional marital counseling. He recommended an out-of-state Pastoral Care and Counseling Center.

It was excellent advice. The center was one where we could go, both together and separately, for professional marital counseling. We were promised that our case would be kept absolutely confidential, and it was decided that we would stay in the private rooms on the secluded grounds.

In public life, one adjusts as much as one can, to living in a fish-bowl existence. But it was felt that, in order for healing and wholeness to take place, we would have to get away to be assured of confidences being kept, to feel safe, and to be able to put our souls together again without the glaring spotlights of publicity.

In one of our first sessions together, in early spring, the counselor assessed our situation and recommended that we try an in-house separation. I personally hoped that it would help us to better understand and to effectively deal with some of our problems, but after a few months of the secret (even to our children) attempt at separation, it was obvious that it wasn't working. Communications were no better and the relationship grew even more tense, increasing my pain levels substantially. A few therapy sessions and months later, the counselor felt we should end our unworkable California in-house separation.

Finally, by October of that year, while we both were staying at the center and having daily sessions, our counselors recommended that we should formally separate because of the conflicts, differences, and trauma between us. It was also advised, starting with that day at the center, that we should begin the separation that afternoon with one of us relocating in another room.

No physical pain, no matter how complicated or prolonged, was ever as excruciating as the emotional pain of that day. The walls of my denial and refusal to see the pain of my life as it really was were torn completely down. They vanished! I saw my existence for what it really was; and, in doing so, the unbearable realization hit in full force. I understood fully that my thirty-two-year marriage was in all likelihood gone . . . over . . . I also realized, because of my denial, I had not been able to see or admit that the marriage had been finished many years earlier.

I remember vaguely thinking that we had been like two very young trees when we were first married, planted side by side. But in a short matter of time, each of us had grown in different ways with different growth patterns and in very different directions. The years had intensified those distinctions, and with the addition of TMJ pain, they had grown into destructive and conflicting patterns.

The two of us sat in that terribly painful session, trying to listen to the counselor. I was dazed with shock—as anyone is who experiences the end of denial and abruptly begins to face reality—and numbly, I tried to concentrate on the counselor's reasons about the justification for our unconditional separation. Then, piercing through my deadened senses, I began to realize that the counselor's voice was becoming more intense and I was hearing some heavy words. I was further stunned to realize that those words of accusation, rebuke, and blame spoken by the counselor were being directed at me. It seemed my whole personhood was under attack. I felt humiliated and destroyed as the counselor's remarks continued. The steady barrage of words kept hitting me like a thousand sharp-edged stones.

I wanted to jump up and shout how unfair this all was, but I couldn't seem to move and my breath was coming in short gasps. I knew I was only hyperventilating, but I couldn't speak out and I felt I was strangling to death. There was an intense pain in my chest and my TMJ pain (on its twenty-third consecutive day) was approaching the unreal level of four, with vomiting and diarrhea a matter of minutes away.

Struggling, I finally managed to get up out of the armchair where I was sitting and, as I started for the door, I said that I *had* to leave and that I was on the verge of hysterics. The counselor ordered me to sit back down. Because my spirit and everything else inside of me was so broken and demolished, it was easy to do as I was told.

It was very hard to follow what happened next, for much of it remains a dark blur in my mind. Since pain of any kind often makes us very hard of hearing, I wasn't able to follow the discussion too well. But somehow, I was aware that the counselor had mercifully left me and the denigrating appraisal of my life, and had gone on to another matter—that of suggesting ways to facilitate our formal separation at home in California. In a moment or two, the counselor looked at me and said, almost pleasantly, "I think that's good. Is it acceptable to you?"

"Is *what* acceptable?" I asked.

"Your moving out of the house."

"Who, me?"

"Yes. You."

Then, from the other side of the room, across from the counselor, I heard, "I am not moving out. It's my home . . . and I'm not leaving."

I protested, "It's my home, too!" I had invested thirty-two years of my life—in energy, time, decorating, creativity, money, and much, much love into this home for our family. I pointed out that rarely was the woman, in a trial separation, the one who moved out—that their "automatically agreed-on decision" was cruel and that I had no place to go. But none of what I begged or pleaded made any difference. No amount of words or logic changed anyone's mind. It was settled. I was the one to move out and I would have to find some place to stay for the undetermined length of separation time.

Remembering that moment now, I'd like to believe that the thought behind the psychological approach used in that session was believed by the counselor to be the best and the most effective for us and for our severe marital strife. Possibly the methods used were well-intentioned, even sincerely done, and not meant to lacerate my whole being. However, the wounds inflicted by the conversations in that particular counseling session still ooze with pain from time to time and, since they seem to be taking a very long time to scar over, I wonder if they'll ever heal.

When the session was over, I stumbled back to my room in what had to be the highest, most intense pain of my life. I wandered about for a few moments, then checked my suitcase to see if I had any medication for the pounding, raging pain in my head. I had nothing but a few aspirin. I didn't bother taking them, for I knew they would do no good. So I wept, paced the floor, and tried to tone down the loud moaning which was involuntarily escaping from my insides.

All the life was being whacked out of me. I was somewhere between being too stunned to breathe and not caring whether I did or not. Often in the past, when the pain was unbearable, I had longed to die—just to escape the pain—but never more than at that moment. To this day, it is only by the staying hand of God that I did not use the razor blades in my makeup case.

I was still in my room crying and close to uncontrollable hysterics when a new unworld blow struck at my viscera. In my effort to make some sense out of everything, and in spite of my tears, I reviewed what I could remember about the counselor's words concerning the details of our separation. The plan we were to follow called for me to return to California on the following Sunday. It was settled that I'd move my personal things out of my Del Mar home on Monday. As I thought it through, the word *Monday* triggered off the realization that Tuesday, the following day, I was scheduled for surgery at Scripps Memorial Hospital for the removal of three skin cancers. Because of my splintered emotions during counseling, I had completely forgotten about the surgery. The unknowables and unquenchable fears about the skin tumors, whether they were malignant or benign, were in themselves very frightening. But the thoughts of having surgery, leaving the hospital, staying down in bed as quiet as possible for two weeks, and *not* going home to my bedroom with its familiar surroundings, were unimaginable to me. I have no words, even though I've written many books, to describe the emotional devastation of that dreadful afternoon.

A knock on the door of my room interrupted my sobbing. After I opened the door, I explained my tears and begged him to move out of our house. "Please," I cried. "Let me go home to my own bedroom after Tuesday's surgery." But I realized that the decision made in the counselor's office was positively final.

A few hours later, I took a long walk around the grounds of the Pastoral Care Center in the beautiful early evening twilight. I forced myself to walk, to put one foot in front of the other, in order to ease the heavy weight of despair. I was frantic to try and eliminate the pain suffocating my heart. I hoped that by absorbing some of God's beauty in the surrounding countryside, I could find some meaning to the intensity of my suffering. I tried to pull a measure of healing from the deep green leaves of the giant oak trees and the herd of delicate brown and white deer feeding in the adjacent meadow. But not even the peaceful tranquility of that warm evening would make sense or bind up the stabbings of the unworld's knife. Everything in me was hemorrhaging.

Unanswerable questions poured through me. What could I tell my dear and precious kids? How would this affect their own marriages? Would they hate me? Would they somehow understand, or would they simply write me off as some kind of unwanted disappointment? Would they still love me? What scars would this leave on them and my grandchildren? And how would I be able to carry on with all the additional responsibilities and financial obligations of a syndicated radio broadcast? Was my ministry and my calling ended? Did God have any use for me, and would He turn His back on me, abandoning me if I left the marriage for a time of separation?

I was so consumed by the shocking agony of this new unworld trauma that I was unaware that the levels of my jaw and head pain were slowly lowering. Late that night, when I finally crawled into bed, I remember thinking for just a flash of an instant, "That's strange—my head doesn't feel as bad as it usually does." But I could not sort out the details, so wearily I fell into a very deep, dreamless sleep.

By late morning, I woke slowly, as usual, and the sensation in my whole body was so incredibly weird and different that I thought either I had snapped, and what little sanity I had was gone, or I was in the process of dying. In either case, I lay there praying that God would give His "angels charge over me." There was absolutely no physical pain. None whatsoever! I mentally checked out my head, my whole body, down to my feet and it was unreal—*nothing* hurt! For a long time, I just stayed in bed enjoying the new sensation and trying to make sense out of it. I finally got up and cautiously dressed. I was afraid I'd do something that might trigger off the pain cycles again. But even after I'd eaten breakfast, the pain did not come back. All that day in the center, I was free from pain. I did not understand it nor did I believe that it would last very long.

The undeniable truth is that it has now been almost three years since I have had any extended period of extreme pain with my TMJ.

Looking back on it now, I know that when the counselor decided on a separation for us as a means of working our the marriage, that physical separation caused the stress levels to be drastically affected and reduced. I still have TMJ, and always will, but by removing myself from the intense conflicts of my marital relationship, the negative stress factors were removed and the pain levels dropped dramatically. On occasional days when I do have pain, it is manageable and pain control is accomplished by fairly simple means.

I am still amazed at what awful things stress can accomplish. I hardly had time to enjoy the relief from jaw pain before a new unworld ordeal became reality; and little did I realize that one of the last decisions made at the counseling center by the counselor and ourselves, before we left that final weekend, would hit my life's work and ministry with such crushing force.

On the last day at the center, the counselor felt that we should give our relationship as much time and privacy as possible. So we agreed that neither one of us would tell anyone about our decision to separate. Certainly it was my understanding that hopefully—without any outside interference or additional crisis—the differences and wounding processes in our marriage might be better understood and possibly some sort of reconciliation could be reached.

However, that was not to be.

The unworld dealt another stunning blow and continued to ricochet around me for the next several months. I never knew where it would hit next. Of course I now know that repeated shattering is part of unworld patterns.

On Sunday, before I got home to California—and less than twenty-four hours after we agreed to tell no one of the separation in the hope that some restoration would take place—my pastor was told, after the morning service, that we were separated and erroneously advised that I was getting a divorce.

In less than three months after our agreement at the counseling center to not tell anyone of the separation, to give our marriage a chance of reconciliation, all but three of my speaking engagements were cancelled for the rest of 1984 and all of 1985 through 1986.

It was clearly obvious I was to be excommunicated out of the Christian evangelical world. A few people who heard the "news" about me were the exception and kept completely silent, but most every Christian leader whom I had known or had worked with washed their hands of me as if I were a small piece of rotting fruit, and they did so with unseemly haste.

One author told me a few weeks after my return from the counseling center that the word about me was out: "Joyce has leprosy—don't touch the leper!" It must have been true, for I was instantly untouchable. The rejection letters and phone calls from Christian leadership started to pour into my office.

I lost more of my already depleted spirit and heart in those weeks and months. But most sad was that the marriage lost all its chances for a reconciliation. Cancelling any opportunity for even dialogue, much less healing.

It was over at that point. We had further counseling with other counselors in California, but it was to no avail . . . it had become a lost cause. And once our separation became public knowledge among the rest of the ministers and Christian leadership, it was as if I was tried and convicted and banished . . . with only God knowing the actual facts. My sentence called for me to disappear, as several authors suggested, for two to five years. No one suggested a sabbatical or a leave of absence—just the command for me to *GO*.

A short time later, and it is a matter of San Diego County court records, I filed for a legal separation. I had not dreamed that I would ever be separated; but I knew if I stayed in the marriage any longer, I would not survive the depression and the stress, so I chose separation. Furthermore, at that time, *divorce* was still a word that was absolutely unthinkable and unacceptable to me.

However, two weeks after the legal separation papers were served, my attorney informed me that a divorce action suit had been filed against me. In those moments, the most unworld word and event *divorce*, became a reality. I had to see life as it really was—now there were no denial walls . . . all had crumbled. . . .

Pain

Extraordinary afflictions are not always punishment of extraordinary sins, but sometimes the trial of extraordinary graces.

—Matthew Henry
1662–1714

5

I am writing to each of us who has suffered unbelievably in our own private unworld hell . . . whatever that "hell" might be or has entailed. The idea here is not to form a "poor-me-pity-club" and simply lament together over our sad and tragic circumstances, nor is it to play "Can you top this?" and try to outdo others by suggesting that one's unworld crisis is of a greater significance than another's.

No, the high priority goal of this writing is to bring a measure of understanding and wisdom about the unworld ordeal, a measure of healing for the immense inner suffering, and a cup of hope for today and all the todays out ahead. It is my prayer that these words will help us all to center down about our attitudes toward unworld tragedies, and our responses to others who find themselves suffering in their unthinkable happenings. This writing is also about our ability to hang on to life or sanity, and our need to find some meaning in the pieces of our shattered unworld brokenness.

Now, fortunately or unfortunately, in order for us to relate to each other, I feel I should share some of *my* unworld agony. I must unzip my life and expose my heart. So this means writing about my unthinkable experience—divorce, and I find this chapter most painful.

While I do have strong feelings about marriage, these pages are not meant to be a happy marriage manual, and they are not a how-to book for recovering divorcees. However, because of my own journey and because hundreds of people have written asking me to write about divorce (its reasons, its devastation, and its recovery plan); and because, in three years, I've read as much as I possibly could about marriages, separations, and divorce . . . there are deep chasms of sadness within me over the complicated issues involving the marriage relationships. One would have to be very insensitive to others or be unaware to deny that pain and suffering are being endured in marriages at epidemic levels, even for the most dedicated Christian couples. In fact, I am convinced, from private surveys taken at various churches and retreats, plus my own volume of mail from a cross section of many people, that a large majority of Christian couples, if privileged with anonymity, would answer "yes" to the question, "Would you get of your marriage and end it right now if you could?"

In the back of your mind, take a secret poll of the couples whom you know and determine how many you'd estimate would bring closure to their marriages if they could. What's even more scary . . . ask yourself the same question about your own marriage. As awesome as the truth is, I believe it's time to face the unsurfaced facts that Christian marriages suffer just as readily as secular ones. One woman, a Christian bookseller, recently wrote the following thoughts to me. "Some of us understand that, even in Christian marriages, there are misfits or problems that seem to have no solutions." She went on: "Stress, mental cruelty and emotional blackmail can sap your strength. Believe me, I know."

How sad it is for anyone, especially for some of us from my generation or older, who are expected to choose while we are still in our teens, *one person* out of the whole world for the rest of our lifetime. I say that is sad because what does anyone really know about themselves at that age? I certainly didn't.

Who knows or even understands their personal destiny which lies within, or what talents and gifts the future will reveal? Yet this is the *precise* time of life that we are to commit ourselves to one person and marriage vows *until* our death.

If it's true that every seven years our tastes change, even in colors, fashion, design, food, etc., how can we so blithely and fearlessly sign up for a fifty-year marriage . . . knowing so very little about ourselves, much less the one we are about to marry? Actually, there are more interviews, paperwork, and intensive credit checks when one obtains a three-year car loan or a twenty-year home loan than there is for a marriage; a marriage, incidentally, which is started with the beautiful vows and promises to love, to honor, and to cherish for the next fifty or sixty years.

Make no mistake about it, my heart absolutely thrills for the person who either waited until they found the right man or woman or who felt no misgivings about their wedding day, or who simply, through a stroke of good fortune or timing, married a Mister or Miss Right! It's beautiful to observe a couple like this, who *still has* a wonderful relationship together even after many years.

My Hungarian grandparents were a rare and wonderful couple. They had a special lifetime love which gave me many heartwarming memories. Over the years, as I observed them and other healthy and well-suited couples, I believe they shared some character traits in common.

My grandparents had vast amounts of respect for each other's personhood, gifts, and abilities. Even their humorous remarks and little inside jokes were *not* at the expense of the other; nor did they jibe or dig at each other, calling it "only teasing." They seemed to publicly praise the other's strengths—preferring to deal with whatever weakness that existed privately.

Also, they had an uncanny sensitivity to each other's

needs. They sensed the right moment for nurturing, comforting, or defending the other. My grandfather was the ears, the eyes, even the English language, for my grandmother who lost all her hearing during her first weeks in America. They related to each other by their love; and, as nearly as I could tell, it seemed to be a love without score cards . . . a rich love based on mutual trust which continued until their deaths. I will always cherish the memory of my grandmother, the morning of Grandpa's death, when she looked up at the ceiling above his empty bed and cried out in her Hungarian English way, "Oh Papa, vy you go and not take me?"

But, dear reader, how long has it been since you have been present to view such a loving couple? And, if you did have a chance to observe them in private, did their attitudes and responses toward each other remain the same as they had in public? Can you name a lot of "well-married" couples with very healthy personal relationships—or are you like I am, hard pressed to come up with only a few?

In my mail, the burning question repeated over and over again is, "How have you survived?" And the next question which inevitably follows is, "Tell me, how can I survive and heal?" I'm afraid it's my heartrending experience to know that the unlisted number of couples who stay in bad, emotionally destructive, abusive, or dead marriages . . . far exceeds those who do have healthy, loving, and working marriages.

It also seems to me that Christian couples stay together—trying to adjust or work things out, or just believing that everything will magically be wonderful, for a far longer time than any other couple. I believe that's why, for so many years, the divorce statistics were generally lower in the Christian community. We took pride in the fact that divorce did not devastate the Christian family nearly as much as those couples represented on the national average. We were also asleep, or pretended not to notice that many Christians were locked into terribly troubled, even abusive marriages.

It is my feeling that most Christian couples who stay together in an oppressive or turbulent marriage do so for two very important reasons: their concern and consideration for other people and their awesome fears.

Many couples stay together because they are concerned about the physical care and emotional protection of the children involved. Some remain together believing that to bring closure to the marriage would hurt their spouses or themselves too much. Other couples keep together out of consideration for their religious testimony or church position or ministry. Still others share their joint concerns for their financial interests, political appointments, or for their professional or business careers.

The second reason people stay in an ailing marriage is because of their fears. They fear rejection, they fear being alone, they fear the uncertainties of lost security, or they fear that nothing will change (a horrible fear because they feel the problems won't go away no matter what happens, separated or together). But a large percentage of ailing Christian marriages stay together because of the agonizing fear of all these four little words:

"What will people think?"

What will my mother, father, child, relations, church and Sunday School class members, pastor, boss, co-workers, associates, friends, or community think and, then, how will they respond to me and what will they say?

We are all so highly vulnerable to this insidious fear of what so-and-so will think or say. It is not wrong to *care* about how others will respond to us. We would be cold, insensitive unemotional robots if we *didn't* care. But to *fear* what others think or say, and be controlled by it so much that we stay in intolerable job positions or even in marriages, is psychologically and spiritually sick. In fact, our staying only drives emotional destruction at a faster rate.

Sadly enough, the reasons for staying in a bad marriage are numerous, but none so compelling as our concerns *for* others and our fears *of* others.

I have understood and known, from many conversations with people over the last fifteen years, that almost everyone who goes through the hellacious experience of divorce describes it as the most horrible ordeal of their lives. No wonder we stay locked into marriage because we know or sense that the alternative is *too* painful to face. We know, too, that very few people are able to bring closure to their marriages without one or both parties being vindictive or deathly destructive. It seems to be the nature of the disease. But my recent experiences have shown that, as unbearable as divorce is for most people, the Christian couple faces a double measure of pain. There is a side effect that is usually denied, but its reality is worse than death.

For the Christian, not only is the divorce a living, ongoing hell, but during the time preceding and following it, when the couple is the most seriously wounded, a new and torturous episode begins. Their emotions are repeatedly stabbed by the rejection, criticism, and ostracism which comes from the church and the body of believers. This additional wounding brings an unbearable *second* unworld hell on earth.

As nearly as I can tell, the most contentious issue, at least as it was brought up to me over and over again, has to do with the church's stand, their stated or unstated opinions, and their "rules" associated with the breaking of the wedding vows. I believe the underlying reason for the stigma which is still strongly attached to divorce is the issue of making or breaking a solemn vow. We Christian couples face a horrible dilemma here at this point, for it is as if we have been entrenched in a rigid dogma that commands, "No matter what destructive thing is ongoing in your marriage, the unchange-able rule is . . . *do not for any reason break the marriage vows!"*

So we stay, year after year, in a marriage whose vows of loving, honoring, and cherishing have already been repeated-ly broken and smashed.

Only a few weeks after my separation, in 1984, I remem-ber a phone conversation with a friend. I was stunned to hear him tell me, in several different ways, that the intensity of marital strife I was going through did not matter—only that I must stay in the marriage because of the marriage vows I had made. At one point, he said, "Joyce, you have no higher prior-ity than to *keep those vows*. Why don't you stop your work, go home, be a·wife, a mother, and a grandmother?"

Since we were both Christian leaders and authors with our own ministries and callings, the moment was *almost* amusing. I thought of the bus commercial slogan which ad-vertised, "Take the bus and leave the driving to us." Did my author friend really think I should stop writing and let others do it, and did he think I wrote books for the royalties or the "glory"? I asked him what I was to do about my godly calling to write and my well-defined mission statement? He wouldn't deal with that. In fact, he changed the subject a bit and said I should disappear for several years. Not once did he concern himself with the agonizing issues at stake in my mar-riage nor the emotional pain we were all going through . . . I was repeatedly told I had to *keep the marriage vows*.

I remember sobbing into the phone and pulling myself to-gether enough to say, "I just can't believe that Christ died on a cross at Calvary for *'marriage vows.'* I believe he came, died, and rose again for *people*. Hurting people like me, not dogma, institutions, or vows!"

Before our conversation ended that day, my friend sum-marized what he believed about marriage. He ended by let-ting me know that he felt it was a woman's job to keep those vows intact and to make sure a marriage ran smoothly and worked. Since I'd put that goal at the top of my priority list for thirty-two years, I meekly asked him, "How long is it my job?"

"For as long as it takes," came his confident reply. And then, in a voice the tone of which implied I was overreacting to all of this, he chuckled a bit and added, "Oh, Joyce, we serve a great God and He'll take care of everything."

Of course, silly me! All I had to do was keep the vows and God would take care of all the rest! I'm sure there is *some* truth somewhere in that simplistic kind of thinking; but there I was, hemorrhaging from every orifice of my body, while he offered me a small platitude band-aid and ended with a pep talk about my "duties" and my "exaggerated" fears. He was unable to hear my heart that day so it is no wonder that now, after almost three years, I have not heard a word from him.

What is anyone to do when, after everything has been tried, when all the prayers are prayed, when God does not send the sought-after miracle and when, to "keep the marriage vows" means staying with invalid vows which have already been broken in unnumbered ways?

For me to have followed the line of thinking that says we are to *never* break our vows and we are *never* free to bring closure to a troubled marriage except for "adultery or being unequally yoked," would have meant certain death. In my own case, staying in the marriage would have increased the stress levels, or at least kept them dangerously high, which would have eventually accelerated the physical pain in my life. And there is no doubt in my mind whatsoever that a few more months, or even a year more, of the excruciating physical pain and I would have been forced to have used my escape route—that of taking my life. It would have been the only alternative, the only viable choice left open to me.

Christian leadership and the body of believers put a very

high and holy priority on the making and the keeping of vows—especially those marriage vows. *I do, too!* But I wonder, when are we going to deal with vows which never should have been made in the first place, which are badly made, or the vows which are already gone?

Isn't it somehow possible to be even more careful and conscientious about the importance of marriage vows . . . without being blind to the reality that some vows were never "the real thing" and some are damaged beyond repair?

Maybe first I ought to ask, is there such a thing as a bad vow or a broken promise? My guess is that there always have been poorly made vows and there always will be.

How can we read the story of Jephthah in the book of Judges without remembering the very tragic vow he kept and should have broken? Jephthah was the son of a prostitute. Consequently, as a young boy, he was run out of his own homeland by his half brothers . . . only to grow strong as a renowned warrior. Eventually, he was asked to not only be the commander and chief of the army, but to be the king of the Hebrew people back in his former country.

As king and commander, he led the army to war and he vowed to God that if God helped him and Israel to defeat the enemy, then he would—as the heathens did—sacrifice something dear to him as an offering to God. Jephthah vowed that if God would give him victory and peace that when he went home, he'd sacrifice the first person who came out his house to meet him.

The eleventh chapter of Judges reveals that God *did* give Jephthah victory and then recounts the shocking story about a vow which should have been broken.

Read the story as it describe's the king's homecoming:

When Jephthah returned home his daughter—his only child— ran out to meet him, playing on a tambourine and dancing for joy. When he saw her, he tore his clothes in anguish,

"Alas, my daughter," he cried out. "You have brought me to the dust. For I have made a vow to the Lord and I cannot take it back."

And she said, "Father, you must do whatever you promised the Lord, for he has given you a great victory over your enemies, the Ammonites. But first let me go up into the hills and roam with my girl friends for two months, weeping because I'll never marry."

"Yes," he said. "Go."

And so she did, bewailing her fate with her friends for two months. Then she returned to her father, who did as he had vowed.*

However noble or worthy the king's vow had been, it was a very bad and tragic vow, and he should have never kept it.

I believe if Jephthah had taken his bad vow to God, God would have accepted the king's reasoning about breaking his vow and released him from keeping it. One has to wonder, though, what Jephthah was thinking during his daughter's two-month absence, and why he still did not change or break that fatal vow.

It is a rare instance that one should go back on one's word, promise, or vow ... but it appears that there *are* those times when a vow is wrong and should be broken.

The marriage vows made before God and man begin with "Dearly beloved, we are gathered here ..." and they go on to several beautiful promises. Those vows are, indeed, vitally important. We give our word and it is our responsibility to keep those promises. They *are* sacred and holy. But our ability as humans is flawed—both in the "marriage" and "keeping" departments—and when we find ourselves in the unworld experience of disintegrated vows, we need someone to receive us with understanding and grace.

------

*Judges 11:34–39, *The Living Bible.*

116

I believe we *can* bring our kept vows as well as our broken vows to God. He and He alone knows the facts, the circumstances, and every little variance in our lives, and who but God has the wisdom *and* the grace to accept our humanness. Just today, I read a prayer of confession written by Dr. Lloyd Ogilvie, and one line stands out:

> We often have cared more for principles than people, rules more than responsible love, standards more than sacrifice. . . .

When unrighteous vows must be broken, the God who does know all our circumstances forgives us for making the vow in the first place, gives us courage to do what must be done, and heals our memories . . . loving us, even providing a shield of grace for us, in the midst of our remorse and stricken spirits.

I still do not believe divorce is a desired option, especially for the Christian; but there are times and situations when divorce is the only alternative, unavoidable, and a prerequisite for human *survival*. I respect the people who sincerely believe that marriage vows must be kept intact at all costs and that, *no matter what*, the couple should stay together until death parts them. I wish I could see it in such black and white terms, but I can't.

I don't want to be misunderstood here, so I need to say that I am not giving anyone license (as if I could) or making a case for people to break their solemn vows or even to treat those vows lightly. What I am saying is that it is possible, with the human error factor, to enter into a bad vow. It is also possible for us to go before God, without the fear of being rejected and turned away. God does understand.

Then, too, there's the matter of the sixth chapter of Genesis.

> And the Lord was sorry that He had made man on the earth, and He was grieved in His heart.

And the Lord said, "I will blot out man whom I have created from the face of the land, from man to animals to creeping things and to the birds of the sky for I am sorry that I have made them."

But Noah found favor in the eyes of the Lord.*

Can you read this account and miss the message? God made a decision, later was very sorry for what He had chosen to do, came close to destroying *everything* (but changed his mind), and then took drastic action to revise His course. No, I'm not saying that God indiscriminately breaks vows. I am trying to point out that we can trust God to give us understanding and grace because it seems clear, in Genesis 6, that even *He* changed His mind about something He had chosen to do. His justice and fairness are *perfect* and so is His forgiveness and grace.

There have been some Christian leaders who have stated loudly and clearly their belief that—because Christian women listened to me and read my books—if I divorced, I would be saying, in effect, divorce is perfectly acceptable. One leader phrased it as my giving thousands of women "license" to seek divorce and destroy their families. *I am doing no such thing!*

I would not wish for the most despicable man or woman on the face of the earth to suffer through a divorce. Or, as a friend said, she wouldn't want divorce to happen even to Hitler. The pain of divorce is beyond belief.

It would be cruel of me to ever give careless license (even if I could) to anyone about their marital relationship. I definitely do not recommend divorce as *anything* but an extreme survival solution. But when I see a marriage staying alive while one or both of the people involved annihilate, tear down, and self-destruct each other ... I know something must be done. Something must either heal the brokenness or

_____
*Genesis 6:6–8, *New American Standard Bible*.

end the slaughter. Nobody wins in a destructive or dead marriage. It's a total no-win situation. How can God be served or glorified by our puny reasonings, those reasonings which refuse to face and deal with the emotional or physical abuse in our lives, and prolong and produce such destructiveness?

I can hear you asking was there "abuse" or "conscious or unconscious destructiveness" in your life, Joyce? My answer is yes, of course there was! I'm willing to bet that no one in their right mind ever says, "Because we have a *few differences* in our lives . . . we have decided to separate or divorce." I was amazed to hear one young Christian author say, after two years of her own marriage, "We all have little misunderstandings in our marriages—I don't see why you don't stay in your marriage, Joyce, and try to learn to live with them."

Let me say this as loudly as I can.

The filing for separation or divorce, coming to "grips" and facing emotional or physical abuse or the abuse of neglect, or dealing with the terrible conflicts in our relationships, going to marital counseling, knowing in the first year of marriage that everything is wrong, or staying twenty or thirty years in a marriage in the hope of change and reconciliation . . . these are not simple "misunderstandings" . . . but are *complex issues which tear one's soul to shreds.* And, believe me, the choice to separate or divorce comes *only* after a very long time of anguished, flat-on-your-face agonizing before God.

Of all the divorced or separated people, especially Christians, that I have had dialogue with, not a one of them has ever talked of having some "trivial problems," or related some "incidental" idiosyncrasies of their spouse; nor did they have a casual, "Hey, what's the big deal?" attitude. What's at stake here is not some small controversy, some tiny tempest in a teapot . . . it is an unbelievable fragmentation not only for the couple but for others as well. Somewhere I read that a divorce directly involves and touches at least twelve people within the immediate family and other relatives for every couple.

I would be lying or denying truth and covering up if I said there are no big issues of conflict, no physical, emotional, or mental abuses, no destructiveness in marriages today . . . including my own. And God himself knows I did not want to go through the unworld ordeal, nor did I want to talk about anyone's marital strife—much less my own.

However, over and over again, I've been asked or written:

- How have you survived?
- Please tell us how you are.
- How are you coping with the divorce?
- How do you handle Christians rejecting you?
- Who will *admit* to a troubled marriage within Christian leadership?
- Who will talk to us about mental and emotional abuse?
- Who will speak up for me in my bad marriage? I am married to a church leader who is a good Christian.
- We need a spokesperson. Will you be the one to write about the nagging wars going on in our marriages—both the cold, silent and dangerously heated wars?
- Please write about spiritual abuses. I can't speak about my own marriage because it means confessing about some horrible things in our "picture-perfect" marriage and because of my husband's church position.
- Won't someone speak to me about what I'm going through? My pastor can't (or won't) believe my pain. My best friend won't talk to me because she says, "I'm not going to take sides . . . I love you both." And all my parents say is, "What will our friends at church think?"

Every day in my mail, or by phone, I deal with people's questions and the agony that pushes their pens across the pages or shows up in the strain of their voices. And one word which comes up over and over again is the word *abuse.*

As Christians, we are *beginning*—but only scratching the surface as yet—to admit that there are things such as physical and sexual abuse happening in our world within *our* families. But that newly awakened awareness is only the tip of the iceberg—for lying deeply buried underneath are many more hidden destructive abuses. There are various kinds of abuses happening in marriages and in family circles today. As tragic and crippling as physical and sexual abuse behavior is, the word *abuse* is not limited to those two alone.

There is mental abuse, the abuse of enormous stress, the abuse of emotional blackmail, spiritual and submissive abuse, verbal abuse, the emotional abuse suffered in our own childhood, even the abuse of manipulation or neglect. Saddest of all is the fact that, because some of these abuses do not leave obvious "outward" scars of evidence, an abuse like any one of these can go on—undetected for years—and can even be perpetrated in the name of love, marriage, *and* Christianity.

There are also numerous ways to be unfaithful in a marriage; but, here again, our society and the Christian world only deals with sexual infidelity. It is a common practice to overlook or deny unfaithful acts except adultery.

In the case of Christians who follow Christ's teachings, there is not one kind of adultery, but two; and both are just as much a sin. Often we judge someone on the basis of physical adultery alone, especially if they are caught at it, forgetting our Lord taught that adultery committed in the *mind's* eye and heart is *still* the same thing: adultery. We don't want to admit and deal with the fact that a person can be unfaithful mentally, emotionally, and even spiritually ... and never sleep with someone outside of their marriage.

I wonder when we are going to come to grips about the damage inflicted by emotional and mental abusive behavior? When will we see that, while these are invisible acts of unfaithfulness, they *can* annihilate a person's spirit so much that the marriage cannot possibly survive?

Recently, a letter arrived from a young woman who is familiar with these hidden abuses which go undetected. She wrote,

> I think *emotional hurts* are harder to accept because there's no X-ray to confirm brokenness, no visible blood. But they're there, aren't they? Sometimes physical "breaks" seem kinder. As a society, we deal with the tangible a lot better than the abstract, as you are too painfully aware! If we were to get in a head-on crash and wind up in ICU on machines with IV's, there'd be cards, letters, flowers, pastoral visits, and prayers! With emotional head-on collisions, we don't hear the music anymore . . . we are left alone . . . with God.

I have another burgeoning concern about these invisible abuses and, because of some firsthand evidence, I am compelled to write of them. We all are aware that visible scars are left by physical and sexual abuse, by some diseases and surgeries, by vehicle and industrial accidents, by crime incidents, by weapons of all kinds, and by wars . . . so we tend to lump the scars of any abuse on the doorstep of *physical* wounding. So much so that we manufacture a myth, a made-up theory which insists that emotional abuse is almost always invisible, and that it does *not* leave physical scars. But it's *only* a myth.

Just this past week, a friend sent me some pictures taken after I had interviewed her on my radio program three years ago. There is one picture of both of us in the studio just before we taped her *very* tragic unworld story. There are several other pictures of her as she is today. The difference three years of gradual healing have made in her *physical* appearance is astounding!

Hidden emotional and mental abuse *can* and *does* show itself in very physical ways. When I look at pictures of myself over the past ten years, and especially the picture on my vocal album of three years ago, I can see the physical and emotional pain as clearly as if I had a sign with a neon-lit arrow pointing it out over my head. Hidden or secret abuses can do many things to our bodies. They can aggravate a disease already in progress or trigger off high levels of pain in the most vulnerable spot of our body (in my case, my jaw). They can cause pain which will contort the eyes, wrinkle the face, turn hair grey, bow the back, stoop the shoulders, clench the fists or jaw, and grind teeth at night. These and many more "physical" and definitely visible things can happen with emotional, mental, and spiritual abuses as well as all the other abuses. We must not ignore the damage that these "invisible" abuses *can* cause.

One other important word on emotional, mental, and spiritual abuses. Your unworld experience and mine usually involves much interaction with one person or a group of people. We need to deal, myself included, with the fact that the person or the people who were involved who may even have generated our unworld crisis, probably participated in it—*not* because of their being a bad person, *not* because their heart's intent was not good, but to a large degree because they were in their *own* terrible unworld circumstances.

It is possible that the ones who seemingly cause us the most pain in our lives do it out of the unworld conditions of their own recent past; or, perhaps, the damage goes way back in their childhood. Only God alone knows the tortuous details of their hidden wounds or the abuses which have occurred to them in their unworld existence. If I admit that this unworld condition exists in the heart and mind of the person who is involved in my unworld ordeal—can you not see that the next step would be for me to show that person some grace . . . even some kindness and forgiveness? This giving of grace does not mean going back, covering up our hurts, and pretending that all is fine . . . no, because most of the time, we are not able to turn back the clock on the unworld death, the unworld divorce, the unworld disease, or the unworld disaster which has exploded around us. But it does mean staying sensitive to the possibility that the person who's given us the most pain—may be suffering as well.

Understanding the other person's unworld situation is a large step in our own healing, our own relationship with God, and our own ability to move ahead with living. And it has everything to do with being the person God intended us to be.

The unworld word which has brought total chaos into my life has been, as I said, the word *divorce*. Obviously, my unworld experience may not remotely resemble your ordeal, and my choices and actions could be very different from yours, but the pain—oh, the pain of it all—is simply universal and, more often than not, unbearable.

When the Superior Court of the State of California did grant the divorce, the words of that legal paper read as follows:

> I have previously declared and do hereby declare that irreconcilable differences have arisen between myself and (Respondent), causing an irremediable breakdown of the marriage. I further declare that no form of counseling would assist in the continuance of this relationship.

Whatever the details of "irremediable breakdown" entail, whether it's my marriage or yours, the pain is there. It's real and it's so crushing.

Some marriages die very quickly, others take time. Or, like someone has written about people (but it's true about marriages),

> Some die without having really lived, while others continue to live in spite of the fact that they have already died.

I wish, oh dear, how I wish, hope and dream of the day,

124

possibly soon, when people—Christian people in particular—will try to reevaluate their thoughts, their biases, their
preconceived ideas, their fears, and their condemnation towards the brother or sister in the body of Christ who, *for
whatever reason,* has experienced the breakdown and closure
to their marriage.

I don't know why my mother, Marion Miller, who died in
1966, was as far ahead of her peers and time, but she was. Or
why—although she and many of her generation of women
personally would never divorce—she accepted those human
beings who did go through divorce on the same basis as she
accepted everyone else. She went a step further. Somehow
she understood, though never experiencing it, the pain and
suffering of the divorced person and the havoc it wreaked in
their families.

During the last days of my mother's life, when she was
dying of breast and lung cancer at U.C.L.A. Medical Center in
Los Angeles, California, I took notes of some deeply moving
moments. I wrote,

> Later that day, she opened her eyes, looked at me, and said,
> "You know, honey, there are worse things to die of than this
> (she patted her chest)." From all the suffering I'd seen related
> to her breast cancer, I wasn't too sure I agreed with her. But I
> asked, "Like what?" "Well," she answered thoughtfully, "you
> know, you could die of loneliness, like the kind the newly di-
> vorced suffer from or—" she paused—"worse yet, you could
> die alone—without God." She settled down deeply into her
> pillow. "Yes," she sighed, "that would be the worst death
> possible."*

How did she know anything about the terrible loneliness
of a "newly divorced" person? She was in her late fifties and

---

Mourning Song, by Joyce Landorf. Copyright © 1974. Published by
Fleming H. Revell Company.

coming up to her thirty-seventh wedding anniversary. And why, I wonder, when she was only six days away from her own death, did she think of those people who were "newly divorced?" I have no idea what prompted her words that day—but now, and in the past three years, I do know *exactly how* she would have loved me through my separation and subsequent divorce. My heart spills over at this moment, with love for this beautiful and courageous woman, my mother—a pastor's wife who, while dying, thought there were worse things to die of than cancer . . . and named as one, the loneliness of the newly divorced.

I pray that God has allowed her to see beyond heaven's portals so she can know how much her words have meant to this "newly divorced" daughter of hers. She died over twenty years ago and definitely had a head start on God's type of unconditional love toward other people.

I think one of my mother's secrets was that she never believed *anyone* was "inferior" to anyone else. So she would have never considered divorced people inferior to married people. And because she was quite a Bible study teacher, she would have based her reasoning on some scriptures. It's my guess that this Bible verse would have been uppermost in her thinking as she tried to live and respond to others as a Christian woman and church leader,

> Dear friends, let us practice loving each other, for love comes from God and those who are loving and kind show that they are children of God, and that they are getting to know him better. But if a person isn't loving and kind, it shows that he doesn't know God—for God is love.*

My mother was very reticent to criticize or make judgments on others' attitudes, choices, or responses. I have the

---

*1 John 4:7, 8, *The Living Bible*.

feeling that this verse would have substantiated her spiritual reasonings:

> Don't criticize and speak evil about each other, dear brothers. If you do, you will be fighting against God's law of loving one another, declaring it is wrong. But your job is not to decide whether the law is right or wrong, but to obey it.
>
> Only he who made the law can rightly judge among us. He alone decides to save us or destroy. So what right do you have to judge or criticize others?*

One of the lessons my mother taught me years ago, as she took those seven weeks to die, has come back to me in recent days again and again.

I remember that, just the day before my mother died, my sister, Marilyn, then fourteen, faced the unwanted reality that death *might* really happen. Gently, my mother verified that truth and said, "Marilyn, honey, this disease will not heal . . . I am not going to get well."

My sister's denial was wiped away, and as she stood looking down at Mother, she suddenly flung herself across Mother's body and sobbed out her heartbroken question, "Mother . . . why is God doing this?"

My mother's answer, given so long ago, is very meaningful to me in these unworld days of mine. For she just held Marilyn in her arms and said, very firmly, but quietly, "I just don't know, honey. I just don't know."

In *Mourning Song,* I wrote this next paragraph,

> We may all find ourselves in the place of not knowing or understanding the whys of death, but it is important to realize that when Mother said, "I don't know," she said it without fear, without bitterness and without frustration. Her words,

---

*James 4:11, 12, *The Living Bible.*

spoken so long ago, have tenderly touched my heart to this day.*

When our unworld tragedy forces itself unbidden, unwanted, and unbelievably into our lives, it is possible that we will never know all the reasons for the ugly horror. We just know that the unworld crisis *has* happened. We know we are suffering. We know we are shattered and we believe our survival is impossible. Past this we don't understand a thing.

Some questions may never be answered. Some relationships may never be explained. Some meaning to our pain may never be discovered. Some logical explanation for the brokenness of life may never be discovered. Some people may never understand our choices, actions, or responses. Some may condemn, reject, or criticize us without cause. Still others may consider us inferior, bad examples of Christianity, all because of our unworld experiences. . . . But remember, *God knows us and He is mindful of all the answers, all the raw places of our souls, all of our unworld facts, and all the circumstances of our lives.* It is safe to put our unworld tragedy into God's loving and gentle hands.

Mourning Song, by Joyce Landorf. Copyright © 1974. Published by Fleming H. Revell Company.

BLOOM COUNTY

by Berke Breathe

YES, MR. BINKLEY? ON BEHALF OF THE VOTING MAJORITY OF OUR BOARDING HOUSE RESIDENTS, I'VE BEEN ASKED TO SPEAK TO YOU.

BROTHER OPUS... WE ALL KNOW THAT YOU HAVE COMMITTED PENGUIN LUST.

BUT THE BIBLE COMMANDS US TO HATE THE SIN AND LOVE THE SINNER. AND OPUS... WE ALL **DO** LOVE YOU!

MORE PRECISEL... WE'D LOVE Y... TO MOVE OUT

THANKS.

6

The cartoon before me is just one of a stream of humorous spirit-lifters my friend, Barbara Johnson of Spatula Ministries, has sent to me. I've carried this one everywhere for over a year now.

It shows a worried, tense little man lying on his psychiatrist's couch. The doctor, seated on a nearby chair, is smiling and fairly bursting with confidence; and, in his most enthusiastic manner, he is saying to his patient, "No, no, no! That's just not true. Not *everybody* in the whole world is against you or rejecting you! There are billions and billions of people out there who don't care one way or the other!"

Perhaps reading this cartoon instead of seeing it loses a little in the translation, like a joke in which "you needed to be there" to get the humor. But this cartoon—the worried patient and the over-confident doctor—has warmed my heart and brought me back to a more sane perspective of myself many a time.

Within a few short weeks of the onset of my unworld experience involving separation, I began to feel the annihilating impact of rejection, judgment, and critical comments from my Christian brothers and sisters in church, leadership, and the media. Rumors abounded and bombarded me with amazing zeal and fervor. It was easy for me to believe that "everybody" in the whole world was against me and rejecting me, so it was good that, at the same time, I was reminded that there were "billions" of people, somewhere out there, who *didn't* care one way or another. Often, the cartoon rescued me.

The most articulate and verbal indictments came from Christian leadership people. Each person formed his or her own critical opinion and very few kept silent. To say I was *not* slightly overwhelmed and somewhat stunned by the intensity of angry rhetoric would be a lie. Later I realized that some of the people who were the angriest with me and my situation were the ones who are unhappy in their marriages. I sensed that part of their anger had nothing to do with me . . . but was generated by their inability to bring healing or closure to their own marriages. Perhaps what was most awesome to me was that a number of people seemed to be more concerned with the ominous implications of the *idea* of divorce than with what I was going through, emotionally and spiritually, as a separated and very broken woman.

Hardly anyone seemed willing to believe my feelings, opinions, experiences, or my explanations. The sense of abandonment was so strong that during my first session with my counselor, when he asked me, "Joyce, what do you want from me?" I virtually shouted, "All I want is for you to believe me. *Just believe me!*" The good doctor was kind and quickly explained that when his patients talked of their feelings, there was nothing else he could or would do but *believe* them *and* their feelings. I remember settling back a bit and being relieved to find that at least there—in the counselor's office—I was safe; I could tell how I was feeling and the doctor would not discount, minimize, or even sermonize on my raw, hemorrhaging emotions.

During the next few months, by one way or another, I heard from thousands of people . . . most all of them Christians, and many of them connected in some way with Christian leadership. Now, while I know there is an unsavory downside to any group of doctors, lawyers, or politicians who cover up, support, and go out of their way to protect each other . . . I must say that a little of that supportive-caring attitude from my peers in Christian leadership would have certainly provided a small but wonderful umbrella of relief from the trauma I was experiencing.

One of the few uncritical letters which *did* come at that time came not from leadership, but from a very astute young woman, Jeanette Murphy, of Seattle, Washington. She wrote,

> You *now* know the initial shock of judgments and opinions, the sting of which is unrivaled, paralyzing and often times, as pain-filled as the problem itself.
>
> I beg God to flood you with His grace so that you will "hang on" and prepare yourself to weather the storm of opinion.
>
> Dear lady, dear, dear lady, *hang on*. Please don't let the world win . . . and be crushed by our unfeeling, human indictments.
>
> I have every assurance in my heart that you chose the last possible alternative at the last possible moment.

How true these words were. I knew, as to the separation, that I had gone with the "last possible alternative at the last possible moment." But I was yet to find out how crushed I'd be by the judgments, opinions, and "human indictments."

My world had gone almost, as it were, overnight to absolutely topsy turvy. I did not believe I'd ever see a day in the future when the crises, controversy and "human indictments" would ever taper off or die away.

Part of understanding and adjusting to being a highly visible person in some area of leadership means accepting the loss of personal privacy as something that simply goes with the territory.

It is my guess that when I read the caring letter above, and the line that said I should prepare myself "to weather the storm of opinion," I really believed I could. I felt that, with God's help, I'd be strong and insulated enough to withstand that particular storm. The problem was that I had no idea of how heavy the rains or how destructive the winds would be—in terms of public opinion, wildly inaccurate rumors, and the numerous attempts to defame my personhood.

As I look back on it all now, I wonder . . . How does *anyone*, in the name of common sense, *prepare* oneself for the chilling feelings of loneliness, worthlessness, and the cold isolation of each day? Especially, how do we prepare ourselves for something we've never seen or experienced before? How are we expected to gear ourselves up to face issues and to deal with rejection from family, friends, and former colleagues? How are we to protect ourselves from the howling winds of rampant rumors and charges of being a sinner, or worse, an immoral person from people who know little or nothing of the details of our despair? And then, there's the problem of those who do not say anything at all. How can we endure those deep Siberian silences of loved ones, or people we thought of as old friends?

How, for instance, does a mother prepare herself for the death of her baby or grown child? How do children prepare themselves for the death, divorce, or suicide of one or both parents? How does one prepare oneself for the loss of a home by a flash flood or a disastrous fire? There are many books written about disasters and about the horrible aftermath that comes from them, but rarely do those books give us advice or suggestions which tell us how to prepare for such events.

In reality, I feel there's actually very little that can prepare or protect us as we experience our unworld crisis. When the painful process of closure became a reality—I watched my thirty-two-year-old marriage dissolve. The stream of verbal comments, the unsolicited advice, and the destructive rumors (particularly the rumors that blamed me for what I did to break up my marriage) filled me with an acute sense of bereavement for the immense losses in my life. I was left without hope, without joy, and certainly without any sense of a future. "Preparing" myself was impossible.

I now have experienced firsthand the true awfulness of the unworld havoc. So you would think it all would have taught me some ways of handling losses. Yet, even though I wrote a book on death and dying—*Mourning Song*, in 1974—I still was not prepared, three years ago, for the unworld agony; or, this past week, for the death of my father.

Knowledge alone, understanding the dying process, reading about how others coped with their losses, or attending workshops on working through our grief experiences are all excellent roads to recovery and certainly have their well-defined place in our healing ... but, they are usually after-the-fact. They don't teach us how to specifically prepare for loss, for that *unthinkable* thing which could never happen to us, for critical opinions and remarks made publicly and privately, or for our responses of anger, resentment, or despair.

I have kept and stored many boxes of mail that came during my separation and the years that followed. As I read some of those letters *now*, I can truly see and hear the difference between the critical and the caring ones. But back then, when I was going through the main vortex of my unworld crisis, hearing and seeing the positive and healing messages was a very, very difficult thing to do. All I could hear was the loud clanging noise from the voices of rejection. Kind and loving letters and phone calls tended to bring some balance to my upside-down world but, by and large, the ear-piercing voices of criticism drowned out the soft, gentle healing words.

Last week, while we were attending the Christian Booksellers' Convention, several dear and valued friends commented that they had written to me in the early times of my despair. Then they indicated that they were disappointed that I had not responded to their letters.

I apologized and told them about the boxes of letters which did not reach me for several months; but mainly, I realized that their letters reached me at a time when all my senses were numb. I was, in a way, paralyzed. I remember that writing a grocery list was a major task and reading any more than two lines of a newspaper was exhausting ... certainly *hearing* those dear friends was almost impossible and responding was beyond my strength levels.

In retrospect, because I was a highly visible Christian leader, I should have known that there would be a flood of mail. Letters came from my radio listeners, peer group authors, family, friends, readers, pastors, missionaries, and from Christians all over the world. An amazing number of phone calls came into my offices, too many to keep an accurate count; and, only because of a specially dear staff of people, were the calls taken, letters opened, and most of them answered.

As I said, the rejection came from many Christian leaders, from some of the Christian publishing companies, from Christian radio stations, Christian booksellers, from Christian friends and relatives. The torrential downpouring of verbiage and the storm of indignant public opinion raged on each day. When the letters arrived from very old friends and co-workers—whose intent was good and whose motives were well meant—they explained their judgmental and critical accusations away by saying it was all meant "in Christian love," or, worse, "in tough love." They hardly ever offered any grace to me or asked *what* was happening; they only wrote of what they *thought* was wrong. Very few people had any of the actual facts straight, nor had they taken any time to really listen to my heart. Over and over, I thought of the cliché, "My mind's made up—don't confuse me with the facts!"

Today—separation, divorce, remarriage, and three years later . . . I opened the mail to find a welcome letter from a young wife and mother who explains that she wishes she could write "pages and pages" to me, but she and her husband have five sons (all under ten years of age). Still, she writes,

> I have tried to write this for one and a half years—ever since I heard your marriage had broken up and a local church had taken your tapes and books out of their library! Recently, I learned of your remarriage and wanted to send all my prayers for God's blessings on both of you!
>
> My marriage is only still together because of your ministry and God's grace through *you*!

Then she tells me what several of my books and tapes have meant to her, and closes by saying,

> Please write a whopper of a book about those who judged you harshly because of your divorce and remarriage. Our churches are loaded with divorced and remarried . . . they need your God-given gifts. . . . "

Of course, it is not my intent to write a "whopper of a book" about people's negative responses to me—but having lived and survived the immensely negative hailstorm of rejection . . . perhaps you, as you go through your own unworld ordeal, can be comforted, can be given a measure of hope, and can be a little more whole by my sharing here.

Two months after my separation in the fall of 1984, after most of my speaking engagements had been cancelled, when many wild rumors about my marital problems were circulated and believed, and when one person after another laid much of the blame and responsibility for the failure and breakdown of the marriage on me, I came dangerously close to stepping over that faintly indistinguishable line between sanity and insanity.

Each day was an exercise and struggle to keep from going over that line. Desperately, I wanted to die; and while I did not keep track of all the times I tried, I know I almost succeeded.

Once, even though the thought of death by drowning terrifies me, I walked down to the beach, late at night. My intent was to walk into the ocean waves and let the Pacific coast's notorious undertow carry me out and beyond . . . but, even at that hour, there were a number of groups of people on the beach and I was afraid they might feel it their duty to rescue me.

One time, around four in the morning, I put on an old jogging suit and started downstairs to try the beach again. But as I got to the bottom of the stairway, it was as if an invisible arm barricaded my way. I don't remember how long I stood there; but eventually I gave up trying to get past the unseeable presence and went back upstairs to bed. I remembered a line from someone who had remarked that it took more courage to stay alive than to take one's life. Yet, for me, that was not true. I did not have the courage to die—or was it rather that God and a few of His children kept me from my own destructive hand?

Too many times to remember, my publisher and old friend, Francis Heatherley, spent hours on the telephone calling long distance and patiently pulling me back from my own grave site. Sometimes, he would just call my name over and over. He would softly say, Joyce, Joyce, Joyce . . . " and it was as if he were pleading, "Come back . . . don't go way out there . . . come home . . . Joyce, Joyce . . . stay, stay . . . don't go. . . . "

So somewhere between God's invisible intervention,

Francis, and a few friends like Clare Bauer, Joanne Letherer, and Dr. Cliff Penner, I was tenderly and gently compelled to stay here a little longer. But I was most reluctant. There were a few others, during that time and even later, who *did* reach out in great concern to me, but because I covered my emotional agony so carefully, most of them did not realize the depths of the struggle raging within me. Nor did they know how difficult it was for me to hear their concerned voices through my shock and numbness.

Three months after my 1984 separation, I was barely staying alive, much less coping too well. I had no idea that the unworld experience goes in patterns like that. I guess I always thought that when you suffered a terrible blow, it would be a short matter of time before you picked up the pieces and moved ahead with your life. But what did I know?

At this time, I remember one day particularly well. I had received yet another scathingly accusative letter from someone I thought was my friend, and I'd taken a phone call at the office from someone else—again, whom I thought was a friend, and I had been shattered once more. I'd hoped that there was nothing left to be fractured; yet, there I was, with more broken bones, bones I didn't even know I had.

Late that night, the coastal town of Del Mar, California, turned December cold and a steady rain drizzled in off the ocean. I was trying to sort out things and was desperately weary.

Reading *anything* was difficult, but I was trying to find something to read that might hold my heart together and nourish my soul when I picked up Frederick Buechner's book, *A Room Called Remember**. There, in his book, I found both the holding and the nourishing I needed. I remember

---

**A Room Called Remember* by Frederick Buechner. Published by Harper & Row, Publishers, Inc. Copyright © 1984.

that night, laying Buechner's book down and thinking about his room called remember and how he got there. My reflections started a chain of thoughts and questions about the rooms of my own life. I felt like I had stepped from the warm, comfortable room called "remember" to realizing that I was being shoved and pushed into a *very* different sort of room . . . a room, for me, called "rejection." I picked up my pen and hoped that, by crystallizing my thoughts and feelings on paper, I might be able to understand some of the unworld process.

I wrote steadily into the early hours of the next morning. It was a most arduous task because I was feeling the crushing weight and full trauma of others' rejection. Especially heavy and difficult to handle were the letters and phone calls from people I loved, respected, and with whom I worked. The hardest of all were the stinging tirades from those dear ones in whom I had invested large amounts of my love, time, and life. It was the heaviest weight in the world. Add what felt like a truckload of raw hurt, an iron cauldron of steaming anger mixed with resentment, large boulders of sharp-edged fears, solid concrete blocks of despair . . . and you have a fair idea of my mental and emotional state of anguish.

These were my soul thoughts as I poured them on paper that night. Perhaps you, too, after what you have gone through, know each and every feeling expressed here:

I've been sent to my room, like a disobedient child and without my supper.

Oh, I'm perfectly aware that the whole world will get along quite nicely, thank you, while I'm gone . . . but somehow, that doesn't ease my pain too terribly much.

I've been sent to my room with the stern admonition to stay there until I'm ready to say I'm sorry. And, I'm to think long and hard about how bad I am and what I have done.

I've been sent to my room, but not before the guilt-provoking rebuke, "When will you learn to be obedient?" has whistled through the air, aimed like an arrow shot straight for my heart.

I've been sent to my room. It's the room called rejection.

I've been sent to my room to try and figure out what it is, exactly, I've done. What is so horrendously bad? The separation? The possible divorce? What? Am I being sent to this room to be chastised? Is my punishment because the "sin" in my life is gigantic or is it because it is I, a woman and a highly visible author, who commits the "sin"? Which is it? And, I wonder, who says that a marital separation is a "sin" in the first place?

I am trying to keep warm, but the room of rejection is so cold. The shivering of my body and spirit is shaking my faith, my hope, and my peace into tiny fragments. I frantically try to bind up the splintered pieces of my soul in my coat of Christianity, but they spill out and seep through the seams in the fabric. I'm getting colder.

I keep trying to find reasons for staying in this room, or mostly, I guess, I keep trying to find reasons for staying alive . . . but I don't seem to be able to come up with any. The single wish to disappear grows into a multitude of wishes for death to come and rescue me.

I keep trying to see where my brothers and sisters in the faith are coming from. What does all the rhetoric of these good Christians mean? What's their logic, theology, or purpose in the hateful and cruel things they are saying? But I can't figure it out. The light coming through the crack at the bottom of my door is very dim . . . and no illumination lights up my brain with insight.

I keep trying to hear the still, small voice of God within me, but the volume of the sound speakers outside my door are blaring and shouting about how I've failed my husband, my family, and have destroyed my marriage. They rant about how disappointing I am as a leader and role model for so many women. About how invalid my books and tapes are now. About how unusable I am now, to people and even to God. "Especially to God," they clamor.

This room is empty except for me, I think. But I really can't tell. It's so dark in here. I wonder how many of God's children have languished in this room before me? Or *died here*? I wonder how they got through the seemingly endless days and nights? Or did they feel exactly like me? Did they want to break out of this room, run to some international crossroad and shout, "Wait a minute! This is unfair! Let me tell you my side!"

I wonder if others ever stopped crying, if they ever felt safe enough to go to sleep . . . if they *could* sleep and, if they somehow got out of this room, did they see the dear faces of their loved ones again? Or were there any loved ones left?

I wonder if they ever felt the strong, silent presence of God and did they sense His everlasting wings underneath them? Or are God's wings under us just a myth, just something authors write about with a great flourishing of their pens?

I wonder, Lord, when you were in your room of rejection, the one marked "Gethsemane." Was it like this room is for me? Presumptuous thought, I know, that you and I might share in each other's suffering . . . but I still wonder. Or was it completely different for you, Lord? Are our crosses and times of crucifixion so different?

I wonder if anybody ever survives their suffering in this room?

Maybe some people *have* been released, but do they leave in mute numbness with shock gripping and squeezing their already lifeless souls in its silent vise?

But, is it possible that some people have left this room . . . transformed? Perhaps they came in broken and battered but they've left as gentle victors, taller giants, and unconquerable warriors. Maybe they are still able and eager to follow truth, and still eager to be God's person? Or is this just a misguided, pathetic little hope of mine?

God, will I ever get out of here? Will the public and private storms of rejection end? Will I leave this room like those above . . . unfaded, undisturbed, and undaunted in my determination and unmovable in my faith? Will I truly leave this room transformed like they . . . warriors of the faith?

They, who followed the tiny bright light of God's truth in the viscera of their souls and mind when all other lights either blacked out completely or blinked now and then, beckoning in other unknown directions.

They, who like the many people listed in Hebrews 12, somehow managed to shut their eyes and ears against the clamoring storm of responses and trusted God by totally blind faith.

They, who in the tradition of Abraham, did what they knew had to be done, remained faithful to God . . . even though everything about their decision was foreign to them.

They, who believed the Lord when he said, "Neither do I condemn thee . . . ," like the nameless adulteress who went away, knowing she was forgiven and loved.

They, who with the soul of the denying Peter, or a doubting Thomas, knew that the reality of this terribly cold room is to know also the God of forgiveness, the God of understanding, the God of mercy, and the God of grace!

Dimly now, I sense God's presence. . . .

"Hello God? Are you here?
I hope it's you. . . .
But I can't be completely sure.

Have you come to take me out of this room?
have you brought the fire of your love to warm my freezing spirit?

have you come to sit and visit a spell?
have you come to rescue me?

God?
Goooooooooddddd???????"

The room called rejection differs slightly from "God's Waiting Room," as I described it some years ago in books, tapes, and the film series. The difference seems to be that when we are *waiting* on God, at least we know on *whom* we are waiting. We feel the silent and sometimes verbal encouragement of the other people waiting in the same room. We share a kind of camaraderie; and, for some reason, our time of confinement in that waiting room does not feel quite so bleak and endless.

Another difference between the waiting room and the rejection room is that often in *waiting* on God, our personhood, our character, our self-esteem does not appear to be maligned or annihilated by someone else's responses or their avoidances. Maybe that's true because people bad-mouth people. God does not.

It's been almost three years since that rainy night in California. I'm not in that room called rejection all the time now . . . only at certain periods and for indefinable and unregulated amounts of time.

Speaking of time, I've grown allergic, as it were, to the cliché *"Time heals all wounds."* Time *can* be our friend; time can give us breathing space from the unworld crisis; and time can ease our hearts and minds into increments and measures of healing . . . but time does not, and cannot . . . heal all wounds.

Towards the end of the first year of my separation, about six months after I wrote of the emotions I felt in the room of rejection, the unworld crises were still exploding around me on a daily basis. Until I went through my papers, I had forgotten that I'd written a piece on the "invisibility factor" of the unworld experience. It's strange, but time had dulled some of the heavy blows of pain in my memory. As I reread my own scribbled handwriting, I wept and realized once again how intensely painful rejection can be. I now understand that continued rejection eventually rubs out your recollection of who you are. My feelings about my identity were nebulous indeed. Suddenly, while I knew intellectually who I was—and that my name was Joyce Landorf—emotionally, I felt totally invisible.

I recall the day I was shopping in Alpha Beta, my local California grocery store. A woman came up to me and asked, "Aren't you Joyce Landorf?" Her question wasn't that unusual, but my instant response surprised me greatly. I answered, "I was."

Losing my sense or feeling of identity is something which continues to perplex me. I still struggle with the identity problem. I've learned the unworld experience can wipe out our sense of belonging and replace it with deep feelings of abandonment faster than I can write about it. "Just who am I now?" is a valid question when we have massive grief losses and we are so terribly wounded by people's rejection.

Even now, living in the heart of the Texas Bible belt, I reside in what appears to be a very unforgiving town, and I have felt the sting of rejection over and over again.

The paper I wrote on the invisibility factor was prompted by an extremely painful incident. I'd been crushed by a co-worker, who walked by my table in a restaurant but would not speak to me, even though I called his name. While I was feeling more fragmentation and invisibility than ever before, I came home to write,

> Grief steals like a cat burglar, pillaging and ransacking my soul in the darkness of each night. Every morning, I awake to find a little more of me stolen. Bits and pieces of me have vanished and my feelings of emptiness cannot be measured. It

feels very strange and painful to be alive and invisible at the same time.

I feel invisible when I discover the loss and sudden withdrawal of love from some family member who previously seemed supportive and comforting.

I feel invisible like today with [my co-worker] and last week, in the same restaurant, with four women at a nearby table who recognized me. They talked it over and then turned away, refusing to speak. I do not exist; I am invisible ... which, of course, really says over and over again to me ... I am worthless and of no possible value whatsoever....

I feel invisible with so many of my former publishers. In last night's mail, a woman told me she called one of my publishers and asked for my mailing address. She wrote, "I was shocked. They acted as if they had never heard of you."

I feel invisible when I learn that if my name is mentioned, a large percentage of people in my world (God's people!) act as if they never knew me, and as if they never put me up on an unrealistic pedestal in the first place. My feelings of invisibility are not born out of some egotistical need of mine for that pedestal, or even out of the loneliness for it, but rather for all the severed ties and the broken relationships. After so many years of keeping me up on some kind of man-made pedestal— now they wish I'd disappear. It's easier to deal with a problem person if they just go away. But I cannot disappear except in the minds of others.

I feel invisible and nonexistent when I think about my mission statement ... which clearly spells out that I will, to the best of my continued ability, bring (by whatever means of communication) the healing love of God to the hurting people of the world.

Somewhere in my early childhood, I knew that I was a bit unconventional. I played with other children, but I enjoyed adults far more and their conversations fascinated me. I didn't seem to fit into too many molds. I also believed, perhaps at my mother's urging, that I was entrusted by God with a number of gifts . . . I do not know *how* I knew that I was called by God to reach out to others in their need.

Once, when I was eleven years old, at home practicing my piano lessons, I sensed the presence of God in the living room with me. When my mother came in a few moments later to see why I had stopped practicing, she saw my tears and asked what was wrong. "Nothing's wrong, Mother," I explained. "It's just that I *will* be God's person. I don't know what He wants me to do . . . maybe it has to do with singing and playing the piano, but I just know God will use me to help people." My mother did not laugh or even think it strange, bless her darling heart. She just hugged me and said, "Yes, Joyce, honey, you will!" I was aware of my "destiny" as surely as one hears a call, sees a vision, or has a dream to be a minister, a doctor, a lawyer, a missionary, or even a scientist or librarian. Reaching out to others and offering a cool cup of water, in God's name, was what I was born to do.

Today, because I feel so invisible, I doubt that calling. Perhaps it's temporary, but today I feel *uncalled*. Maybe especially today because an executive of a publishing company has written me and says, "You have forfeited your right to ever minister again." His words magnify all the hidden inferior and negative feelings I'd *ever* felt about myself.

The feelings of invisibility and the pain of rejection and the adjustment to losing so much so quickly (and I'm not talking of material things as much as the loss of relationships with others) were very hard and forceful teachers. The lessons were—and still are—hard to accept. But, I am slowly beginning to see what I believe are some fundamental truths emerging from these unwelcome and disheartening lessons.

One such lesson-truth has raised itself like a frantically waved red flag in mind. It warns me about my own vulnerability and propensity to become, because of my unworld experiences, a bitter person.

Not too long ago, I began wondering about my own personal bitterness . . . for as much as you or I might wish to escape the bitterness route, that just might not be possible. In fact, I believe there is hardly any chance, given our terrible hurts and humiliations, that we will walk away unscathed and untouched by bitterness. Unworld situations and ordeals are unfair and we are easy prey to the monster of bitterness. However, there is, and always has been, an enormous difference between having a *bitter experience* and actually becoming a *bitter person*.

Anger and resentments over the raging injustices of our unworld suffering can plow and prepare the ground for the seeds of deep, unresolvable bitterness to come to harvest. But it doesn't have to, nor does the unworld experience *always* have to produce a bitter people.

Perhaps there are a couple of reasons why I think I'm on the right track about the bitter experience versus the bitter person.

The first reason is FEAR!

I am scared to death of becoming a bitter person. I am equally determined to use that fear for good. I believe that most people genuinely and sincerely do not want to end up with the withered soul of a bitter person. I know I don't!

I do not feel I am a bitter person; but, in my unworld sufferings of the last three years, I have had many bitter experiences. I've even had whole days when the emotion of bitterness vented itself through my weeping and came close to overwhelming me.

However, I'm beginning to understand that when an unworld crisis devastates us, we should *expect* to feel the harshness, the viciousness, and the gall and wormwood of bitterness. To deny these feelings would be to deny our humanness. We must always keep in mind that if we are to survive, we've got to keep a healthy respect and fear of the power that bitterness has to destroy and devastate our spirit.

I believe also that most of the time, if we *face* and *accept* our unfair unworld situation as a part of life, then we will probably be better able to cope with the grievous events and with the bitterness that often tags along as its unwelcome shadow. But, on the other hand, if we deny or pretend that we have *no* bitterness, then not a whole lot of *anything* can take place. In denial, bitterness can begin to grow like an unseen malignancy inside our souls; and unless it's cut out quickly, it will continue to grow, even metastasizing somewhere else, dooming us forever.

I fear becoming a bitter person so greatly that I am almost paranoid. So, I've made up my mind that I'll admit my struggle and not hide the fact that, out of my hurt, I *am* experiencing bitterness. Hopefully, in this way, I'll be better able to move on, turning the awful experience into compassion and empathy for others. It is well documented that often the quickest way to recover from our most painful losses, our terrible wounds, or the wildly unfair situations of our lives is to reach out to someone else who is suffering. It's proven to be more than merely a therapeutic way of dealing with our own bitterness—it facilitates *wholeness*. The choice between being a bitter person or a compassionate person lies within all of us.

The second issue about having the bitter experience versus becoming the bitter person is

Finding the HUMOR!

Sometimes, I feel we tend to believe that having a sense of humor means being a comedian with quick and witty one-liners, writing humorously like Erma Bombeck, telling a great story or joke, or laughing about each and every bad situation in life . . . but I'm not sure having a sense of humor is any of these things, in reality.

Possessing a sense of humor really means not taking ourselves too seriously. It also means training ourselves to look for and find humor in our daily walk through life.

I did not learn this truth on my own. I had a wonderful teacher—my mother, Marion Miller. Although at first brush with her, you might have missed her contribution to my education and training about humor. She never, and I do mean *never*, understood any joke. I could tell her my funniest story. She'd listen politely and attentively. And, after the punch line, she'd smile brightly and exclaim, "Oh, that's nice, dear. That's very good!" I always knew that, sometime later, she'd pull someone aside and ask, "Now, tell me, what did the last line mean?" So she was not a comedian, nor did she respond well to organized humor, but she had the most keenly developed awareness of what humor could do in life that I've ever seen. She quite simply believed that having a sense of humor meant not taking herself too seriously. I believe she was quite right.

My childhood memories are full of examples of my mother's training about developing a healthy sense of humor. For instance, when I fell and hurt my knee, she was immediately there for me. Sympathetic, loving, and gentle, she would take care of the scrapes and bruises. After she cleaned me up and comforted me for as long as it took—my mother would, in a very tender way, help me to move on and get back to play or whatever. Years later, I was able to articulate exactly what it was she was teaching me, for she left in my memories something like this: "Now, Joyce, honey, you have had a bad fall (or whatever), but we've got it all cleaned up. I've kissed it and put a band-aid on it, so it's probably going to heal and be fine. . . . Oh, yes, one other thing . . . I doubt that the President, in Washington, D.C., will call a meeting on this. . . . So why don't you go back out to play or carry on with what you were doing?"

In other words, she never minimized my hurts, but neither did she believe that my bruised and cut knee was of national concern or interest. And it certainly was not serious enough to merit a congressional hearing.

Years later, as I accompanied her to some of her Bible Study meetings when she was about to teach several hundred women, it never failed—somehow she'd get a run in her hose just as she was getting out of the car. Instead of going into some tirade about how many stockings she had ruined that week, or being horrified at what all those women in the auditorium would think of her hose, she most always looked at her leg and asked, "Have you noticed how they're wearing runs this year?" And then, lifting her skirt a bit on the other leg, she'd add, "Oh, and isn't that clever? I've got another one over here to match!"

That kind of insightful comment was my mother's very balanced, humorous perspective and way of handling everything—from tiny mishaps to the most crushing of hurts. She must have decided somewhere in her youth to try to lighten up her attitude about her own struggles and to train herself to find some humor in those experiences.

I now know that her teaching me to not take my cuts and bruises too seriously, when I was little, put me in a good position to handle, with some humor, the ugly hurts of my life later on.

Seeing our lives and the experiences we have through the filtered glass of humor, I believe, can literally save our lives. And I mean this, whether we are talking of some small embarrassment or of experiences of extreme bitterness.

Several years ago, I was asked to be the keynote speaker in an Evangelism conference for pastors in San Jose, California. Since I was trying to beat a book deadline, it was decided that I would fly up from Southern California, speak, and return home that same afternoon. As usual, when I'm writing, my mind was totally preoccupied with the book. The man who met my plane drove me to the auditorium in a van marked *Billy Graham Associates*; but it didn't connect, nor did it cross my mind, that this was a city-wide Graham crusade. However, when I got to the church, I heard the very familiar voice of Dr. Billy Graham over the vestibule's speakers.

"He's here?" I frantically whispered to the man who had picked me up. (The Billy Graham Associates badge and the name tag finally registered!)

"Yes," he answered, "and Dr. Graham wants to say hello before you speak."

I couldn't believe it! I'd never met the great man, and I never dreamed I would ever have a chance to meet and talk with him. Even if it was only briefly, I wanted to say how much I respected him, how I'd prayed for his ministry, how I'd read his and Ruth's books, and which books had touched me the most. Mentally, I ran over the list of things I planned to say when I met him.

Then quickly, I was being walked down a side aisle to the front of the auditorium; and, sure enough, there on the main platform, up several carpeted steps, a few feet away from me, was *THE* Dr. Graham. He was concluding his welcome speech to six or seven hundred ministers and their wives. When he finished, he received thunderous applause and a wildly enthusiastic standing ovation.

Dr. Graham turned, saw me standing with his associate, warmly smiled and mouthed, "Hello, Joyce."

I thought I'd died and gone to heaven! (Billy Graham's life has always been an inspiration to me, and I respect him tremendously.) Then the next moment, he started down the carpeted steps which stretched out across the entire front of the platform, his hand reached out to shake mine, and I took my first step up to meet him. However, I tripped and fell flat on my face across the remaining steps, landing (you guessed it) at Billy Graham's feet!

For a second or two, I just lay there—partly because I would not let my mind believe this was happening, it was so embarrassing! and partly because my heel had caught itself in the hem of my long, full skirt and I couldn't move. It was the great man himself who picked me up, extricated my heel from my hem, and kept asking anxiously, "Joyce, are you all right?"

All the pastors were still on their feet, applauding, and no one had missed my extraordinary performance. I was mortified. But, somewhere out of my childhood training, I knew right off there wasn't going to be a congressional hearing on this. Laughter would be the only way to survive the situation. So, while I was still holding on to Dr. Graham, who was still asking if I was all right, and while I was trying to get my balance, I blurted out, "Oh, Dr. Graham, I think I just fell for you!" His spontaneous outburst of laughter is, to this minute, one of my warmest memories!

I am not, for one moment, daring to compare a fall in front of seven hundred pastors and the great Dr. Billy Graham to any hellacious unworld experience. Except that I believe when we can see our lives without such terribly high and serious priorities attached to them, and we train ourselves to find the humor in all situations, tiny or tragic . . . it is a sane way to keep the bitter experiences from escalating beyond reason. Humor *can* be used as a positive step towards coping with bitterness, and I most certainly was convinced it can help us to avoid becoming bitter people.

One of the most beautiful things about training myself to find the humor in what could only be described as a devastating experience happened in regard to my work.

Almost every day, after my separation, I received some pretty discouraging letters from publishers, associates, authors, friends, or someone directly connected with the Christian evangelical world.

Most of that correspondence did more than casually rain on my parade, spoil my joy, or make me temporarily feel a little down . . . those letters left my spirit, my self-esteem, and my whole being pulverized beyond recognition. I recall a number of annihilating letters, but four or five specifically. They were loaded with pious judgments and malignant rejections. It was only by the intervention of God, and Francis, that I survived the days which followed.

Those letters severely threatened my sense of integrity and personhood. They made it clear that I was unwanted, unrespected, unusable, and most certainly, unloved. When I reread those letters now, my only questions are: Why did I listen to God and Francis, and why *didn't* I take my life? My life and work were ravaged by those antagonistic letters and it's quite safe to assume that I was in no mood, or of a mind, to find any humor amid the devastated ruins of my spirit! I was far more hurt and angry than I ever dared admit.

However, a day came when I poured out my shock and grief about those deadly epistles to my friend, Clare Bauer. I'd just received yet *another* publisher's devastating and insulting letter. Later Clare related that when she had told her husband, Conn, about the kind of rejection I was encountering, he had, in his gentle way, made an amusing observation. He suggested that if we are going to drop an author or stop publishing a book because of an author's sins, choices, opinions, feelings, or their doubts . . . then we would certainly have to remove David's Psalms from the Bible.

The timing of Conn's comment was perfect. It eased my soul across the painful emotional hurt line and moved me into a place of remembering my earlier training; that of finding humor in the worst episodes of life. Slowly, ideas began to take shape and I began thinking. . . .

Take David's work out of the Bible? You're kidding! What

a startling, preposterous thought! Looking at David as an author, in my mind's eye, and envisioning the Bible without his writings was too unbelievable . . . I began to see and enjoy the humor of it.

Pretend for a moment, you're watching a video starring David, King of Israel and best-selling author of the Hebrew people. Visualize David, as he might have felt, when he received the bad news from his publishers and associates.

Dear King David:

Greetings to you from all of us here at your publishing house.

Word has reached us of your recent troubling circumstances, and we are deeply saddened. We also find ourselves caught in an embarrassing position. For, on one hand we felt proud and annointed by God to do the holy work of a publisher but, on the other hand, we cannot condone the unholy consequences of your actions and continue to publish you.

After numerous editorial and management meetings, we regret to inform you that it will no longer be possible for us to publish your work.

Of course, if by some miracle your "circumstances" change, then that might allow for some adjustments. But until then we cannot publish or promote you or your Psalms.

Please aunderstand you are our beloved king, but we do not choose to be a part of your writings. And we do pray that God will deal with you in a merciful manner.

Cordially,

Amos, Son of Benjamin

Or, watch the video as David reads an editor's letter.

Dear King David:

With all due respect and humility, as the editor of your Psalms, I must say that I am at my wit's end in trying to understand you. How, in the name of all that's holy, have you adjusted your mind to the problem of Bathsheba's adultery and Uriah's murder?

It appears that you don't even feel like you have displeased God. Such a sin! In my mind you have given up your kingly position to ever minister through the Psalms.

May God have mercy on your poor soul.

Sincerely,

Nahar, Son of Serug
Editor

Hear the heart of King David, on another occasion, as he receives a letter from another publisher who is about to publish some of his new Psalms:

Your Royal Highness, King David:

Today we received the dismal report of your "circumstances." We are all shocked and disappointed in you and your behavior.

In your 101st Psalm you deceived us into thinking that you were *such* a spiritual person. Now you have let us down with your personal failures.

As chief scribe of this publishing company I am in a very difficult position. I cannot, in good faith, see how we can go into print with the release of Psalm 86 and the future books of Psalm 102 and Psalm 145.

You have been a valued author with our company, but I feel you should be aware that some of our other authors are concerned. They feel that you, King David, have sinned and sinned against God, so either you leave or they leave. It is as simple as that.

You understand that our decision to not publish you has been a difficult one but one of moral conscience and one made after much prayer.

Some time in the near future I plan to take a trip to Jerusalem, perhaps if your circumstances *do* change, we can get together to discuss your veracity as an author. In the meantime, may I humbly suggest that you get lost? After all, how could you write anything uplifting and meaningful after what you have chosen to do? No offense, king, it's just that now there is no market out there for your Psalms . . . and I doubt there ever will be.

Sincerely,

Japheth, Son of Shem
Chief Scribe

Or, feel with David, after he has written to several close friends in his publishing companies, about the "circumstances" of his life. Now came a couple of responses to his letters.

Dear King David:

The messenger delivered your letter of explanation just after daybreak this morning.

I choose not to respond to it at this time. I trust you understand.

Regards,

Jahab

Then feel David's hurt as he reads a letter from a tiny country where he was to visit for meetings with the high priests:

Your Royal Highness, King David:

We regret to inform you that we are canceling your state visit to our kingdom. Word has reached us of your immoral conduct and we feel, under the present circumstances, that your visit should be postponed indefinitely . . . or at least until we hear of some repentance on your part.

With all due respect, King David, you have sinned against

your God; and to have you appear, especially as the guest of honor at our national banquet, would be inappropriate. It would look like we were condoning your "circumstances," and our kingdom and our temple priests could not afford to be put into that position.

Please know that we hold you in the highest respect and honor and look forward to having some meetings with you at some future time. However, we cannot publicly be seen with you at this time.

Sincerely,

Hadoram
High Priest

Or, see the last scene in this video with David reading a letter from his long-time friend and associate:

My dear friend David:

It is with utmost pain that I must tell you I can no longer represent you as your Royal servant. You have no idea how much this hurts. We have been good friends for years and I respected you and your writings.

However, I am apalled at your relationship with Bathsheba. Also, the ugly rumors about Uriah's death are just too hideous to comprehend. I simply cannot remain in your court. I have spoken to the court council and they agree and understand my position completely.

Do understand that nothing will change my basic love for you, or Bathsheba either, for that matter, but my love is not broad enough to encompass the sins which you both have committed. So until you confess and repent of those sins, I'm afraid I cannot provide you with the kind of representation you want or need.

I will continue to pray for you.

Love in God,

Kenan, Son of Enoch

How grateful I am to my friends, the Bauer's, for providing me with a fantasy look at what could have been a tragic, unbelievable time in David's life. It does help to know that God, who knew *all* the facts about David, did not take away his calling, his gifts, or his ministry to people.

In today's mail, there is an angry, hateful letter from a pastor's wife. It is typed, and over two pages long. Each paragraph tears my soul to shreds.

She tells me a number of things, and ends by repeating an ugly rumor that she's heard from a publishing representative. In capital letters, she writes,

"YOU HAVE DISQUALIFIED YOURSELF TO MINISTER."

Then, at the end of her letter, just above her signature, she adds,

"FORGIVEN BUT DISQUALIFIED."

After I was able to somewhat control my sobbing, I finally remembered God and His beautiful, ongoing relationship with David. How grateful I am, *again*, that God forgave David, did *not* disqualify him or his ministry, and called David a man after His own heart.

Then, a funny thing happened. I'm positive I heard God chuckle. And, in my mind's eye, I saw a telegram. It read:

DEAR JOYCE,

ABOUT THOSE LETTERS.
THAT'S HOW SOME OF MY CHILDREN FORGIVE.
NOT TO WORRY—I DON'T DO IT THAT WAY.

YOURS TRULY,

GOD

Apparently, there was forgiveness and peace made between God and David. Interestingly enough, when you think about it, whose writings do we read or hear most often at the grave side of a loved one—when we are deeply grieved and need comfort more than any other time? That's right. David's twenty-third Psalm. Thank you, God, for knowing all the facts and for keeping your hand on your child, David. Perhaps his tombstone should read:

"HERE LIES DAVID—*FORGIVEN TO MINISTER.*"

In no way am I suggesting that anybody's writings, including mine, could be as powerful as David's Psalms—but what a tragedy if he had been judged, rejected, and thrown right out of the publishing world of his day because of his "circumstances."

The letters and calls of rejection that I have received, and continue to receive, at times are really not so bad, and not quite so painful, if I remember to look for the more humorous aspects involving my unworld experience. Certainly, the pain is never really removed from the wounding caused by the rejection of others, but finding the humor somehow does provide a measure of relief and somehow it eases the hurt. More important, viewing our lives from a humorous perspective can move us a little farther *away* from becoming what we all fear, to some degree or other, a bitter person.

A Room Called Grace

> And God is able to make all
> grace abound toward you. . . .
>
> 2 Corinthians 9:8
> *King James Version*

7

As I reexamine my own unworld holocaust of three years ago, I constantly visualize an analogy which forms itself on the edges of my mind. I can see it now, and it occurs to me that since most analogies break down at some point, and some more quickly than others, perhaps this analogy can put things into a better perspective. Maybe it could work, to some degree, by applying it to anyone who is dealing with an unworld crisis.

It seems that the unbelievable events surrounding the closure of my marriage put me into virtually the same type of choice-filled trauma one encounters when faced with the frightening aspects of a malignant cancer.

Because of my mother's death by cancer, the people who have shared their feelings, and the research I've done on my own, I know this: In order to achieve a cure for the disease or even to effect a possible remission, a cancer patient has to face and make some very difficult decisions.

At some point, the medical oncologist may advise, even recommend, chemotherapy—which, simply put, is chemical (drug) treatment—or therapy by radiation. Often this comes when the patient is in a state of shock about the onset or the recent discovery of the disease itself. Then, as they are moving into the stage of denial and disbelief regarding their cancer, they are informed that if they decline chemotherapy or radiation treatments altogether, it could hasten their death.

At the same time the patient is trying to absorb everything, he or she finds that accepting chemotherapy and using toxic (poisonous) drugs or radiation treatment comes with their own set of drawbacks. Several rather real *and* nebulous issues raise their ugly heads. It's hoped that the patient can move on to a cure, perhaps even to a partial or total remission, but they are exposed and also vulnerable to a whole sequence of mild to severe side effects. More than one cancer patient has told me that those "side effects" of chemotherapy or radiation were almost worse than the disease itself.

In my life, I had the feeling that my unworld disease was metastasizing rapidly—the malignancy was getting out of hand. Was my case to be labeled "terminal"? The word *survival* suddenly became uppermost in my mind. Was I to survive? Did I even *want* to survive? I felt like I was dying, but— with one unworld blow after another, and quite quickly, I reached the place where I did not care if I lived or not. In fact, in some ways, I preferred death because of my Christian beliefs about the joy, the peace, and the painless existence to be gained in heaven. My death wish was very strong, and I desperately wanted to end my life to escape the unworld pain.

The reactions of those close to me, at this time, were especially interesting. Some ignored and denied my suicidal feelings, even when I shouted them out. Others pleaded with me to stay and steadfastly refused to let me go.

However, to my surprised horror, I found that some people—when they finally *heard* me and took me seriously— were theologically, spiritually, and emotionally able to accept my intent of suicide far better than my separation and pending divorce. One person went so far as to tell several people that taking my life would certainly settle all the issues of my separation and make things much "better." I was then, and I am now, appalled that someone could suggest to anyone else, even to an enemy, that their suicide would be a better and faster route to solving their problems. It was pointed out to me, by a couple of Christian leaders, that "removing myself" (their euphemistic term for suicide) had more going for it than living in the evangelical disgrace of breaking my marriage vows.

Sometimes, the conversations ended with, "Joyce, God hates divorce." Yes, I *am* familiar with the Malachi 2:16 reference. However, when I read the entire second chapter, I see a much better picture of what God's message was to His people. Besides hating divorce, that same passage states clearly that God also hates cruel men.

For anyone to encourage another person to take their life, as if it is making the best of a bad situation (or for *any* reason, for that matter), is definitely being a cruel person. Very cruel indeed.

Besides that, I think I hate divorce almost worse than God does! Virtually everyone I've ever talked with who has gone through the searing unworld pain of divorce has felt the same emotion of hate. No one, probably not even an unscrupulous divorce lawyer, loves the demise of a marriage and the uncoupling process.

I am alive today because God and a few of His precious people felt I was worth saving. I owe God and that small band of people a tremendous debt of love for caring and helping me stay alive.

In spite of my wishing to die and be released from the emotional conflicts in my life, and even knowing about the risks and the high possibility of side effects, I finally decided to opt for "chemotherapy," or small doses of poison, as a measure of hope and healing for my unworld ordeal. That chemotherapy came by several different methods and some of the treatments continue to this day.

First, if I were to survive the daily crisis experience and

deal with my constant wish to die, and the depression which is that wish's persistent ally, I knew I needed the intensive care of a psychologist or psychiatrist. So, soon after my separation, I found a Christian counselor whom I believed understood both my desire for a doctor with professional expertise and my need for absolute confidentiality. For the next five or six months, I was in continual touch with him; and those sessions held me together even though the unworld crises were awesome in their annihilation and destructiveness.

A wise friend wrote about the fear we people-of-the-pedestal have concerning our need for therapy. She wrote,

> I'm beginning to believe that the reason so many Christians, leaders, preachers and Bible teachers are so wary about psychotherapy is because of their own insecurities and unconscious fear of exposure to the falsity of their own cherished doctrines.
>
> Jesus said that people hated light because it would expose their evil deeds, and men loved the dark more than the light (John 3). This is exactly what can happen through careful, loving and wise therapy. It is a way to bring to light all of our values and doctrines out into the open, examine them and ask, "*Is this truth?* God, show me your way. Is what I learned growing up really valuable in Your eyes, for your Kingdom? Do I keep it or do I toss it aside and learn something new?"

I know that when chemotherapy treatments are most effective, they either interfere with the growth of cancer cells or prevent those cells from reproducing altogether. The good derived from psychotherapy, in those sessions with a skilled, caring professional counselor, was not unlike the good which can come from chemotherapy to a disease. Therapy illuminated what was *truth* in my life, and sessions like those are still a very viable method of healing the pain of an unworld situation.

Secondly, and as a direct result from the insight I received

from counseling, one of the most disagreeable aspects of chemotherapy for my unworld disease was the knowledge that I
had to risk being open and honest with people—including
my readers and radio audiences—and with God, if I was to get
well. But how do we walk that fine line of honesty without
opening all sorts of related wounds in ourselves, and without
hurting other people who are involved?

I could not, nor would, reveal or explain the details surrounding the demise of my marriage. I didn't have a need, or
find it appropriate, to correct all the erroneous rumors about
me, or to defend myself from all the scandalous accusations.
There was also no desire to use my widespread public forum
to discuss what God and I already knew. However, at the
same time I did not feel, as a Christian woman and leader,
that I should cover up or keep hidden the fact that I was *indeed* going through a hideous unworld experience. An experience which, by the way, *could* and *does* happen to those of us
who least expect it.

So, after weeks of agonizing prayer and a few private conversations with those whom I could trust, I made a decision.
On my own, I made a public statement, in general terms,
about my separation status—both in letters to my readers,
and in a radio program to my listeners.

I should have not been too surprised that, shortly after
that broadcast, many of the Christian radio stations dropped
my program. And, as I've already alluded, most of the Christian publishers followed suit. In all fairness, it must be said
that they had every right to decide who they would allow to
be a broadcaster and who they would publish, and every
right (whether I agree or not) to choose their own method of
handling the news of my separation. Some called my open-
ness and honesty "courageous candor"; others were "appalled," "disgusted," or "disappointed" in me, and could not
get away from me fast enough. A few declared that, as a lead-

er, I should be brought before the church body of believers, disciplined, or perhaps excommunicated ... but no such "body of believers" has ever materialized.

The complicated and lengthy process of shutting down a syndicated radio broadcast with a national ministry, and closing Joyce Landorf Ministries' offices and staff produced a side effect which tore me apart emotionally and financially. Emotionally, I mourned the death of a long-time dream of mine—and broken or lost dreams sometimes die quite slowly. Financially, the burden was just as awesome. I paid off the enormous financial debts of the radio ministry by myself. I felt that I should not let Joyce Landorf Ministries, my own Christian organization, fall into bankruptcy, even though I knew that paying off the debts out of my own funds could mean that I might go into personal bankruptcy. As it turned out, I lost almost everything, and am still paying on some loans; but I am glad now that I went that route and made the expensive sacrifice. The satisfaction of knowing that Christian radio stations, production and advertising people, and my staff members were paid has brought its own unique healing within me.

However, the high price of honesty was tremendous, and the chemotherapy of my candor made me extremely vulnerable to the wildly spreading stories and the escalating rumors regarding my separation. Some felt that because I was a highly visible "public" leader, I owed an explanation to everyone; but I found that the more I answered questions or revealed about my choices and circumstances, the more malicious the gossip became. To some, I could not give enough answers.

I experienced a terrible truth during those days and learned, the very hardest way possible, that when many Christians hear of a couple's separation or divorce (especially if one or both are in a leadership position), they are driven by a basic need to identify and publicly point out who is *at fault*.

I've noticed, too, that when we hear of people in unworld trials, why is it that we, the body of believers, feel led to give our opinions, our reactions, our lectures, and our spiritual recommendations? And why do we particularly seem to have the uncontrollable urge to fix the blame and righteously denounce the guilty party or situation? And this method of dealing with unworld situations isn't reserved for the divorced alone. Perhaps it's the adult or child who has a chemical addiction, the person who is mentally or emotionally ill, the man or woman who is homosexual or bisexual, the teenager who commits suicide, the person who commits a crime, the loved one who suddenly dies or who lingers in a state of living death, the victims of incest, rape, or sexual abuse, or the abusers themselves.

Often I think we Christians are blissfully blind to our own faults, sins, and shortcomings, but we have a remarkable ability to clearly see others' unworld situations as well as—or better than—God himself. When one Christian brother or sister has set themselves up as judge and sentenced another, I've been tempted to ask the rather farcical question: "When did God die and put you in charge of explanations?"

Sadly enough, in the case of a couple who is separated or divorcing, we speculate about who or what *really* caused the breakup and who's to blame. Unfortunately, we rarely keep these opinions to ourselves.

A few days ago, I talked to a recently divorced man. When I asked him how he was doing, he answered, "About half and half." Then he added, "What I can't understand is all the bad things other Christians are saying. . . ." He went on almost wistfully. "I guess I just have to leave it in God's hands." I think he got that right! But saying it and learning how to do it are two different ball games!

I wonder, Why isn't our first response to *anyone*, in an unworld crisis, that of accepting the fact that we don't know the facts? The facts aren't any of our business, and even if we did know all the facts . . . it is God who judges, forgives, and has planned out our days.

With the tremendous number of divorced people around us—in our families, in our churches, and in today's society— when will we see that here, before us, stand two very shattered souls (with a radius touching at least twelve immediate family members) who are presently in the severest of all pain and who need *not* our judgments, but the intensive care of our love?

I believe, having experienced the brokenness of divorce, that we have our absolutely *golden* opportunity to practice what we, with almost nauseating fervor, preach! As caring-dedicated-to-Christ-people, we should be constantly asking, "What Christ-like thought or gesture can I bring into someone's unworld, painful life to let them know they are loved and still of value to God and people?"

I wish I had a nickel for all the times in the past two years that someone has quoted (or misquoted) atheist Madelyn Murray O'Hare's words: "Christians are the only army of people who shoot their wounded."

It seems we all agree to the truth of the line, but strangely enough, I've *never* met anyone who was willing to admit they have actually shot at a wounded soul. Everybody says everybody *else* is doing it.

One of the significant and rather universal truths to be learned about unworld suffering is that while we may have deliberately or unknowingly shot and wounded a soul in the past . . . once we experience our *own* unworld pain, we develop a totally different perspective because *we* suddenly know what shooting the wounded is all about. We *thought* we knew how pain felt—but we've now discovered for ourselves that the pain of being wounded by another is unbearable, and it is *very real.*

I must go one step farther and say that I believe my response to people in unworld circumstances must not be reserved for Christians exclusively, but *must* extend to anyone, anywhere, regardless of religious, political, cultural, or social convictions.

Time magazine just reported Peter Jennings' marital separation. While I do not know him personally, he is my favorite national newscaster, and I felt a deep sadness for both him and his wife. The details of what happened, or who did what, or the whys of the problem have nothing to do with me, nor do they interest me. I only know, from the pain of my own unworld wounding, that I wish I could hug them both, and I wish I could wave a magic wand, making everybody's hurts go away.

I am still smarting over my memories of a few years back when a leading Christian author went through his unworld ordeal. I did not publicly or privately express an opinion, or try to place any blame. Still, I did not see the need, or seize the opportunity, to be the loving, caring Christian I should have been. To my shame, I kept silent.

My silence was certainly not the way Christ would have handled unworld people. From the excruciating experiences of my own painful past, I pray I've learned the powerful truth that my job is not to judge or to psychologically or theologically set everything accurately in its proper place. What I do know is that *God and God alone knows each and every detail!* He knows and understands even every intent of our hearts and minds. So, for this reason, only God is the perfect judge for us, especially for our unworld tragedies. He knows all the details. My job is not to be the judge and jury to others, but to love them.

Thirdly, besides counseling treatments and "honest/ open" procedures, I experienced another form of chemotherapy in my ongoing attempt to survive my unworld crisis.

The course of treatment involved a totally unexpected school of learning—although I should have guessed and seen it coming. It was the chemotherapy of timing and waiting.

The lyrics of one of my most favorite songs read,

> In his time,
> In his time,
> He makes all things beautiful
> In his time.
>
> Lord, please show me every day
> As you're teaching me your way
> That you do just what you say
>
> In your time
> In your time
> You make all things beautiful
> In your time.
>
> Lord, my life to you I bring
> May each song I have to sing
> Be to you a lovely thing
> In your time.

With cancer patients, the length of time, and how often they take their chemotherapy treatments, depends on what kind of cancer they have and which drugs are used. With unworld people, the length of time and how often we go through the scary process of treatments with the potentially new and painful side effects depends on what kind of unworld suffering we are enduring and exactly *which* process God is allowing to take place in our lives.

The chemotherapy of waiting on God's timing and dealing with unexpected crises on a daily basis is one of the most arduous tasks one faces in the unworld process.

About this time, a new series of events and time frames came into view; and, while I now see God's plan and am grateful for each and every *awful* thing, the depressing side effects still made me desperately ill, as it were, all over again. Once more the shattering, the breaking, and the fracturing process began with greater intensity than ever.

In the first six months of 1985, a letter written for me by my secretary to a young TMJ patient traces the path of un-world timing and waiting.

My Dear Debbie,

So very much has happened since we last talked that I hardly know where to start! First, as you realize, the Joyce Landorf Ministries was greatly affected by Joyce's personal circumstances. This resulted in the termination of the radio broadcasts on May 17th, and we are now in the process of closing down the ministry entirely. All the staff has been released, the offices sublet, and we will be officially disbanded as of the end of this month.

It is costing Joyce over a quarter of a million dollars in shut-down costs; all but two of her scheduled speaking appearances have been cancelled with the attendant loss of revenue; and her book royalties are being held against possible book returns; so, in general, this is a time of horrendous pressure and strain.

Her home was sold just last week, with what we believed was a forty-five day escrow, so we thought she had until the end of July to relocate; however, it now looks as though she will have to be out by the fifteenth of July! Because of this, everything is having to be accelerated.

In view of this, Joyce's therapist and counselor, feels she needs at least six months to a year to heal, and that she should move totally out of the state—and rent some place which feels like a retreat center to be alone, to be quiet, and regain some sense of wholeness. At this point, she doesn't know where she will go, or even if she will have any resources left at all—so she is again in God's waiting room, listening for His voice, while mourning the death of her marriage, the death of her ministry, and the death of many dreams.

When my home was sold, I felt as if the last of my roots were not only being pulled up but were disappearing into thin air. The house had been on the market for a long time, and rarely had anyone even looked at it. But, within two days, I received two offers; and, because it was in God's time, the house sold. However, as you may know, there is an adage that says when you solve one problem, you often replace it with a new one. Almost overnight, my relief at selling my home was replaced with my panic as to where I would go. Where would I live? Would I rent or buy? I had never been involved with financial details until I paid the ministry debts, so I didn't even know what I could afford.

I am unashamedly a "nester" at heart, so to see my marriage come to an end, to watch my ministry disappear, to be in mourning and to feel the immense loss of loved ones was one thing . . . but to sign escrow papers was decidedly something else! To pack up what was left of furniture and precious accessories, and to say goodbye to my nest was a horrific ordeal only another "nester" would understand. To have no safe ground, no private sanctuary, no place of my own (no matter how small or how insignificant in size) destroyed my ability to feel any hope, to see any future plan, or to have faith that God still loved me. I remember when I left that home for the last time. Walking out, I felt like I was being dragged down into a thick quagmire pit of despair.

At the same time, yet also in God's time, there was a new and ugly unworld experience which exploded around us.

My long-time friendship with Francis Heatherley (or Doc, as he is known by many) was vilified and denigrated into scandalous grist for the rumor mills.

I've long been accustomed, as a highly visible person, to hearing rumors—not only about myself, but about my peers and associates in the evangelical Christian world. The biblical injunction against the spreading of gossip is one of the teachings that many Christians seem to be able to blithely ignore. Hardly any public person has escaped the inestimable destruction that a rumor can inflict. Whether a rumor is 100 percent true, 2 percent true, or not true at all . . . is not the issue. (In fact, there probably is at least a thin thread of truth running through most rumors—otherwise, we would dismiss them as ridiculous and pay them no mind.) Rumors, true or untrue, dip their pens into the same bottles of poisonous ink.

The malignant rumors about me were unbelievably painful. I doubt that I had any idea just how visible or how well known I was . . . but people from all over the world wrote telling me of the latest Joyce Landorf rumor. As the rumors moved from merely denigrating to virulent, scandalous attacks, it forced me to search my heart and my feelings for Francis. I had to examine the rumors, as to what was fact and what was fiction . . . what was true and what was false.

As I have previously stated, our first reaction to someone experiencing an unworld situation is to try to interpret for ourselves how we think things are and what we believe the exact nature and extent of the report to be. Perhaps there's a bit of gossip in all of us, and when we have to deal with someone's divorce—especially when it's parents, children, or a family member who's divorcing—something inside of us has the irresistible urge to try to figure it all out. I can understand and give those a measure of grace who have a driving need or desire to put people and suffering into well-organized cubbyholes or to set records straight. It frankly feels better when a person can explain or justify an unworld ordeal.

We feel even better when the issues at hand are in the highly definable absolutes of black and white. This is especially true with Christians. For instance, if someone who believes in divine healing is prayed for and then dies of cancer, their death falls victim to the easy black and white explanation of, "They didn't pray hard enough, they had unconfessed sin in their life, or they didn't have enough faith. So that's why they died." We want to explain unworld ordeals in those precise and logical terms.

In an unworld divorce, we begin an immediate search for "sexual sins," and if we find them, we label them as "unpardonable" (which of course they are not) . . . and we seem almost gleeful at dispelling any grey issue by finding an absolute black explanation.

We do not want to face the pain or suffering in the first place; and, where divorce is involved, it's terribly hard to realize that some marriages are *not* made in heaven. What complicates the issues here is that, in our need to set things in an orderly fashion, and in our frantic search for the *truth* of what happened to so-and-so's marriage, we—even we, good Christian people—not only listen to the black rumors, but at times solicit and draw them out from others.

Sometimes, we disguise our curiosity or our gossip in a prayer meeting, when we request prayer for someone and say, "We need to pray for Jane and Tom . . . because, well, you know, they are having problems and . . . and I'm very concerned . . . ah, you know." The unspoken part of the prayer request is often the part that's repeated.

But I believe the worst thing we do in regard to rumors is that we act or respond to the rumor as if it were fact. The need is not to check out all the facts—the need here is to provide *support* for the unworld person, whether we know all the truth and details of the rumor or not. I do not believe I have an obligation or a duty to report the facts or fictions of anyone's unworld ordeal.

In my dictionary, there are three definitions for the word *rumor*. They are:

1. General talk not based on definite knowledge; mere gossip; hearsay.
2. An unconfirmed report, story, or statement in general circulation.
3. Loud disapproval, protest, clamor, or uproar.

Since acting and responding to rumor and titillating stories is not limited to the religious person—see the newsstand and magazine racks, and count all the sensational articles based on gossip or rumors—but extends to everybody, let me say that dealing with rumors in an unworld experience tends to give one quite an education. Perhaps some of the following comments will be helpful to anyone, upon hearing damaging stories told about others.

I am still trying to make allowances for some of the people directly involved in my own unworld experiences, especially those who set themselves up (for whatever reasons) as the unquestionable *source* of truth . . . telling the truth as they perceived it, and sharing their personal feelings. However, this presents a serious problem. Too many times when a "source" voices their *"feelings,"* those feelings are interpreted by others as the whole *truth*. But we know that often, when there is one issue between two people, one person's fact is the other person's fiction. I believe we do God and all people everywhere a terrible injustice when we make up our minds to be the judge and jury to others—based on who said it, or the rumor itself.

Looking back now on my desire to be open and honest and risking the boomerang effect of false rumors as a side effect of my chemotherapy which I *thought* might happen . . . I never dreamed, in my wildest imaginings, that these rumors would be so widespread or would hurt so much. The rumors—especially the ones that people assumed, erroneously, were true—were, and still are, a point of deep pain.

Perhaps it would help all of us, when rumors are circulated about us, to realize there is very little we can do about them once they're started and as they continue to escalate.

Concerning the rush of rumors about me—my separation, divorce, and personal relationships—these are the *facts*, the only facts of which I *am* sure.

First: No one outside of a couple of people really knew and understood the long-standing details and circumstances of the emotional pain and conflicts in my life. And,

Second: Contrary to those widely circulated rumors, sexual misconduct or sins did not bring about the demise of either Francis's or my marriage. As to my feelings, over the years, for Francis . . . only God knows and understands the facts and the timing of the dear and special history of our friendship. I am at peace about leaving that kind of knowledge in God's hands.

I have one regret about the chemotherapy-time of my life, and it has to do with hindsight. I wish back then—especially just after I was separated and was stepping into the hurricane of my unworld crisis—I had experienced my encounter with Wesley. Darling eight-year-old Wesley! I might have made some sense out of other people's accusations, their responses, of the rumors, and of others' silences.

In all honesty, I doubt that knowing Wesley would have changed anything significantly in *other* people's lives, but maybe the time of healing within me would have been hastened a bit. And certainly I could have learned a whole bunch of things out of the lessons that boy unknowingly taught me about *my own* response to hurting people.

I had only two encounters with Wesley, and they were both only a few months ago.

The first was out on the rural country road which sedately

curves past our home. I'd gone out to check our mail box when a young woman stopped her car, rolled down the window, and introduced herself as my neighbor and her son as Wesley. They lived two wide country lots down the oak-shaded road from us.

Before we had finished chatting, I found that Wesley was eight years old, and his mother had recognized my voice and talked about having seen my film series. In the back seat, Wesley was quiet; but once he leaned over the seat and politely waited for a lull in the conversation. He whispered something to his mother who in turn said, "He wants to know if you have any little boys his age living in your house?" I laughed and told him no. Then briefly, I told him of my grandsons, Ricky and James. I promised Wesley that I'd get them together if they came for a visit. Wesley's bright mind, his sweet shyness, and his sensitive spirit drew me to him and, at the same time, made me quite lonely for Ricky and James.

I got a glimpse of Wesley a couple of times after that first meeting as he rode his little blue two-wheeler past our house. But, for the most part, I immersed myself in the complex task of unpacking boxes of books and belongings. I painted walls and stapled fabric to other walls. I moved (over and over again) the furniture in each room, ten or more times, and put up curtains, drapes, pictures, and mirrors.

On one particularly hot and humid day, I was extremely frustrated by some valances I was trying to recycle for my upstairs writing room. I'd measured the material, cut some off, come up short, sewed them back together, and then realized they were too long! And, just as I was remeasuring the window and the valances for the umpteenth time, the doorbell rang. I was annoyed at the way the valances were not giving themselves to my recycling, was hot and sweaty (wearing my oldest, faded, terry cloth one-piece pull-on shorts suit), and was not in too humorous a disposition or given much to being in a hospitable frame of mind. I thought about staying up- stairs, but someone was insistently ringing the doorbell.

Without checking my clothes or hair—I must have looked a fright with that stupid, shrank-too-much shorts suit on—I came down the stairs, but couldn't see anyone through the glass panels in the front door. When I opened it, Wesley pounced out from the side of our front porch and cried, "I'm selling!"

It was my clue, so I followed some unseen script and cried back, "I'm buying!" When I got around to asking what I was about to buy, Wesley's eyes danced impulsively as he told me about a contest at school. He explained that if he sold enough stuff out of "this"—he held up a gift catalog—he might win the prize, which was a "huge, giant teddy bear."

"Are you into teddy bears?" I asked.

"Nope," he said. "I just want to win the contest."

I was thoroughly enjoying our little session, even though the valances were still upstairs and still lying on the floor. I loved the encounter because there are few neighbors in our sparsely populated area, and even fewer adults in our town who speak to me . . . so I found Wesley to be delightful and enchanting.

I didn't have to explain my unworld circumstances, I didn't have to wonder if he'd show me some kindness, I didn't have to worry about how grubby I looked, and I didn't even have to tell him why I was here, what I was doing, or what my plans were for the future. Wesley didn't give a rip about any of that. He just liked me, and I suspected that the business man in the little boy saw me as an easy-sell customer.

We talked and giggled our way through the gift book. I made my selections, but after some more animated conversa- tion, I got an acute attack of conscience and told him I had to get back to my work. He gave me a cute smile, got on his bike, and rode out the curved driveway in front of our home to the road.

My spirits were so buoyant because of our brief encounter that I took the stairs two at a time. My parents had always believed in the seen and unseen presence of angels. And they had a healthy respect, perhaps even a fascination for the verses in Hebrews 13:1,2 which say, "Let brotherly love continue. Do not be negligent in showing hospitality, for in doing so *some entertained angels without knowing it.*"*

Wesley had so encouraged my soul with his childlike innocence, his lack of bias or prejudices, his trust and faith in me, and his gentle, transparent ways that I wondered, Could I have just entertained, there in the front hall of our home, a real, viable angel—or did he just seem that way?

Going back into my writing room and remeasuring those impossible valances pushed Wesley and thoughts of angels out of my mind. I got to my room and remembered that once an old carpenter had told me how he measured a piece of wood many times before he cut it. But his punch line came when he said, "Then after I've measured it one *final* time, just before I put the saw to it, I measure it again." I smiled, because it was the exact place I was on those valances. I knew that to hang those silly things up and have them look right, I'd have to measure and measure; and, after the final measuring, I'd have to measure again!

I worked at it for a few more moments and then, just I was about to measure for the *really* final time before the cutting, the door chime rang again. The valances demanded all my concentration. The moment was too important and too strategic to stop, so I ignored the interruption at the door and went

---

*Hebrews 13:1, 2, *Modern Language Bible.*

right on with my remeasuring. But someone was being very persistent.

Chafing a bit now, because the chime wouldn't stop, I put down my tape measure and looked out the front window. All I could see over the porch roof was a little blue bike lying on its side on our lawn. I opened the window.

"Wesley, honey . . . what is it now?" No answer. "Wesley? Is that you?"

Wesley backed off the front porch and moved stiffly out on to the lawn so he could see me in my second story window. He looked dreadful! His face had gone chalk white, and mechanically he was flapping his arms up and down in a gesture that could only be translated as, "It's all over . . . it's no use . . . I've had it . . . it's hopeless." Gone was the cute little smile, the playful antics, and the bantering. The child seemed filled with stark terror.

For a couple of seconds, he shook his head, opened his mouth, and tried to tell me, but nothing came out. He just kept looking up at me, moving his hands helplessly, and shaking his head in disbelief.

"Wesley, talk to me! Tell me what's wrong," I pleaded.

Somehow he finally found his voice and rasped out, "My worst nightmare has come true! It's my *worst* nightmare! I've dreamed it every night . . . it's my *worst* nightmare come true!"

I demanded now, *"What's your worst nightmare?"*

He shouted up at me, "It's the big black dog next door!" as he frantically pointed down the road towards his house. "He's barking . . . he'll bite me, and I can't get past him to go home. It's my worst nightmare come true. He's gonna get me!"

Before I tell you the rest of what happened with Wesley that day, let me just freeze-frame the moment, as they do in films, keeping the picture and the script "on hold."

Ever since that afternoon, I have remembered the events with clarity and even wonder. Wesley's words, shouted up to me that day, "It's my worst nightmare come true . . ." were the exact feelings I experienced with the unworld happenings of separation and divorce. I think his line embodies the major feelings of panic and fear that we all have at the onset of our unworld ordeal. I can almost smell Wesley's fear . . . it's so real. And I can hear my own voice crying out in terror, "It's my worst nightmare come true!"

Who can we run to when our dreams are not only shattered, but our nightmares come true? Who will take the time to listen? Like Wesley, we rush back to someone we think is our friend, and we pray that person's response will be positive and helpful. But how do we know who we can (and who we can't) go to?

I have thousands of letters from people whose worst nightmare has come true. The unthinkable has happened and then, they tell me, the *real* nightmare becomes a reality—that is the unworld nightmare of people's reactions and responses. Often people are completely stunned (as I was) with the remarks, the judgments, the misunderstandings, or the angry rejection from others. They had expected a response—but certainly not annihilation, invisibility, or defamation of their character.

A few days after my encounter with Wesley, I realized that, at least for me, some important lessons had been taught that day. I pondered it over and over in my mind. It certainly would have been easy to have missed Wesley's message.

It occurred to me that when someone, like Wesley, seeks me out—someone who is deep into a frightening, unbelievable unworld reality, yet trusts me enough to seek me out, sharing the most terrifying thing of his life, the most shocking, damaging thing he ever dreamed in a nightmare-come-true—I am handed a gilt-edged invitation to rise to the occasion of helping a scared, hurting human. I needed to respond to him by listening and believing him. I knew also that my comments and responses to Wesley were vital to his well-being, but I sensed it was just as crucial to my own growth as a child of God to the relationships I either fostered or killed.

Wesley, in his own very dear way, presented me with several illustrations and choices.

Number One Response: *Refuse to get involved with Wesley.*

I could have reasoned that I had given the child enough of my time. After all, I purchased the things for his contest, had talked with him, and that was enough. Now it was best to take care of my own needs, so I could have called down to him and responded, "Wesley, honey, you are a sweet boy, and I'm sorry about the dog next door, but I just have to do my own thing up here. Besides, the big black dog isn't my dog, so I don't know what I'm supposed to do about him."

Many times we have read an account in the newspaper of some person being attacked, robbed, or raped and screaming for help in some way. If the victim lives through it, we are shocked when they report how people came and went, how people stared or casually looked on. But they did not do anything. So many others were curious, but did not care. We are most indignant that the victim's cries for help were heard but unheeded. I've read those stories and felt that "if I had been there" *I* would have helped that person. But, while it is bad enough that we do not get involved with helping a stranger, it is infinitely worse when we refuse to get involved with someone we *know.* Especially when it's a loved one, a friend, a co-worker, or a neighbor who is calling for our help.

Wesley would have *never* understood my silence and my refusal to come down to help him. I wish I'd had that bit of insight after my separation. So many friends and loved ones knew that my worst nightmare was coming true . . . but they, like the priest and the Levite in Jesus' parable of the good Samaritan, looked at me, heard my cries for help, but passed right on by.

Perhaps I should make allowances for people like them. For maybe when my shattering took place, they were *not* aware of the details; or maybe they didn't understand the depth of the panic and fear within me during my nightmare-come-true; or maybe, when I was the most broken, they too were most broken—only their brokenness was kept a secret. For some unknown reason, they would not or could not get involved in coming to my aid, so they kept their silent distance.

I have mourned the loss of friends, family, and associates; but the way out of the maze of grief seems to be, and I firmly believe this, that wholeness comes to my broken heart when I can come to the place of forgiving their silence. The tough part, however, is forgiving people not only for their silent noninvolvement in the early days, but forgiving those who have continued their silences even to this day.

Maybe another significant reason to be extremely hesitant in going to the aid of someone in an unworld situation is the most often raised *risk factor*. We hesitate to risk "what others might think." We can't risk being associated or seen publicly with the divorced person, the homosexual person, or the person who may need us the most because we fear it will look to others as if we are *condoning* their actions. We can't stand the thought of that kind of vulnerability . . . the risk is too great. After all, what will people think of *me* if I am seen with *that person* or *those people?*

I recall my last phone conversation, three years ago, with another Christian author. He had gone to great lengths to spell out for me that he and his wife loved me and prayed for me each day. Several times, he stressed their love . . . he assured me their love would continue, no matter how my marital problems turned out. Yet moments later, when I pointed out that we both knew that he would never allow us to work together, and that we both knew that he had given instructions to his organization to stop recommending me for speaking engagements, or my books and tapes, etc.—he would not respond. He did not confirm or deny "what we both knew." There was just a dead silence. Both of us knew exactly what he was really communicating: "Joyce, you're good enough for private phone calls, but too bad for me to be associated publicly with you."

Another author friend, about this same time, called to tell me I was cancelled as the main speaker for her fund raising banquet. When I questioned her as to whether or not she would level with the audience about my "absence" (the invitations with my name as speaker had already gone out), I was politely informed that they would just say *I* had cancelled.

People were willing to cancel me, but unwilling to take their part of the responsibility to explain the truthful reasons. When I protested that to announce that I had cancelled was not only untrue but unfair, she hastily explained that if she went ahead with plans to have me come and speak, it would look as though she was publicly supporting my ministry, in spite of my separation. She added, "And you know I couldn't do that."

Several times, in the months to follow, I found people cancelled my speaking engagements at their churches or conventions and then announced publicly that I had cancelled because of illness. The inference being that I had let them down or not told them soon enough for them to get someone else.

Just recently, when I was speaking in Florida, I couldn't make sense out of several remarks I heard. People came through the reception line while I was visiting and autographing my books, and several individuals told me they had gone to hear me at a local church, but when they got there, I didn't show up. The audience was told I had cancelled out on them. I could see a familiar pattern of denial and cover-up. Again, it was untrue and unfair. However, *untrue* and *unfair* are very familiar words to a person going through an unworld ordeal.

Today, in the mail, was a letter from a bookstore. It is a beautifully written letter, but the message is incredibly painful to my personhood and to my feelings of self-worth as a child of God.

The executive writes to say that they have chosen not to carry my books in their stores. He explains the decision by talking about their ". . . deep feeling that we should not appear to condone divorce and remarriage. . . ." Then, at the close of the letter, he writes, "Rest assured that no one here is attempting to put himself . . . in the position of judgment or pontification. We harbor no animosity toward any author who finds himself or herself in a difficult situation. Please be assured that we love you both and care about you."

The message is very clear, and hits its target . . . wounding deeply. When he describes a person's finding oneself in a "difficult situation," I know he does not understand one single thing about unworld suffering, unworld pain, or unworld trauma.

Condensed, his letter means: "Just between us, we love you. However, we choose not to sell your books or be seen publicly with you because it might look bad for us." Again, it's the I-love-you-privately-but-not-publicly concept.

Thank heaven Jesus didn't mind risking what other people thought of him, so He talked to the hurting. He didn't find it necessary to love privately, only behind closed doors, but He *chose* to love everyone—from the righteous to the out-and-out sinner publicly and in full view! Nor did he worry that being seen or eating dinner with well-known sinners meant He was condoning or supporting their sin! Come to think of it, Jesus didn't get into trouble for associating with the good people of the day, but He caught all kinds of flack for appearing or being seen publicly, eating or talking, with the bad ones and the sinners. His critics made much of the guilt by association theory, which must have been around even then.

I'm so glad that Jesus responded and got *very* involved with the unworld people of His time. I wonder . . . when will we accept our responsibility to the unworld people of *our* time? When will we see that a broken, hurting person is at the place of their greatest need? More than any other time of their life, they must have someone here on earth who will say, "I'm here. I'll be 'God with skin' to you. I'll walk through the fire with you. I'll bind up your wounds. I'll sit beside you in church. I'll go places with you. I'll help you through. I don't care who knows it. I don't care who sees us together. I don't care what others think. According to the New Testament and the repeated examples Jesus gave us, I am going to involve myself with you while you are suffering so!"

Why is it that, most of the time, we do the opposite of what Christ did, with unworld people? We freeze them out of the ministry, we take away the communion table, we write them off our guest lists in our social life; and, as if we are frightened to death for fear someone will say we condone sin and sinners, we do the most untimely and unthinkable thing . . . we abandon our brothers and sisters in the faith. Then, perhaps in order to justify our hypocritical actions and responses, we explain that we are not really abandoning the suffering person because we "still love them privately and personally." It is unchrist! We make hollow words of Tertullian's first century comment when he said, "See how these Christians love one another."

I can only guess at the complexity of reasons as to what holds us back from being true New Testament people or from learning the truths Jesus taught, by example, in wholeheartedly rushing to the aid of the broken.

Historically and culturally, in Jesus' day, the dregs of humanity were prostitutes and tax collectors. Jesus astounds me! He did not *attack, discipline, correct,* or *condemn* any one of those highly visible sinners in the entire New Testament records. As I read about all His encounters with people, I find that the major part of His three-year ministry was a single-minded dedication to interacting and involving Himself with people—

- Jesus, in front of the whole town of witnesses, invited Himself to lunch at the home of the tax collector, Zacchaeus!
- Jesus did the unthinkable thing, by even speaking to a despised and hated Samaritan ... much less a Samaritan *woman* ... then He offered her a cup of everlasting water so she would never go thirsty again!
- Jesus, to the woman accused of adultery, publicly—in front of a whole group of men—does not give her a sermon on her sin, or her need for remorse and repentance; but, rather, asks her where all her accusers and stone-throwers went ... and, finding none ... He tells her He doesn't accuse or condemn her either. In essence, He tells her she's all right now with God, she should go home, she should forget her past life, she should get on with living as God's child, and that she should sin no more!
- Jesus publicly asked for and got Matthew, the tax collector, to be one of his closest associates. An apostle, a former tax collector? Goodness!

But, in my mind, the most astounding moment in Jesus' ministry of involvement with unworld people came during the time of His death by crucifixion. Two criminals were placed on crosses, flanking Jesus. One of the men cursed God before he died; but the other man cried to Jesus for help, asking, "Jesus, remember me when you come into your Kingdom."

What moves me to the very depths of my being is that Jesus, in the midst of the excruciating agony of His own unworld dying, replied, "Today you will be with me in Paradise. This is a solemn promise."*

Incredible! Jesus involved Himself with everyone He met . . . whether it was with the huge crowds of people, the single man, woman, or child; the righteous, the sinners, the criminals; the sick and contagious, the handicapped; the religious leaders, the rich, the poor; the most renowned, the most scandalous, the lowliest of unknowns; or with another, while He himself was in the throes of dying.

I don't know what message you get from Jesus' words and continued involvement with people—but for me, especially when I read about the way He reached out and tenderly cared for the thief on their mutual day of crucifixion, the clear impact of His involvement is astounding. To me, it says that even when I feel as if I'm dying, even when I'm too broken to move, even when I've lost all hope, all direction, all identity . . . then, I must reach out to others!

I must not care what others think of me. I must not trust a theological scenario which shouts, in one way or another, "Don't have anything to do with THAT person!" I must not be afraid of the consequences of public opinion. I must not worry if others misconstrue my involvement as my *condoning* the hurting person's behavior, choices, or sins. I must not weigh the facts about someone's unworld ordeal. I must not judge their circumstances or fear the consequences of my actions before I make a decision to help.

What I must do, if I would be a true child and servant of God, is to train myself to listen for the cries of the desper-

_____
*Luke 23:42, 43, *The Living Bible.*

190

ate and to *get* involved and care for others when they are in the furnace of their unworld holocaust, no matter how seared and scorched I am by my own unworld fires.

But, back to Wesley's unworld nightmare come true.

Number Two Response: *Minimize Wesley's fears.*

I could have yelled down from my isolated ivory tower writing room, "Wesley, you're being ridiculous! Stop it, this instant! After all, the dog is *only* barking . . . he's not going to bite you. You're being silly about this nightmare business . . . now snap out of it!"

When I was Wesley's age, my Dad was pastoring a church in Owen Sound, Ontario, Canada. The church's rented parsonage was a third floor one-bedroom flat. I slept on an army cot in a small glassed-in porch off the living room. It was the only time I was truly afraid of the dark. Well, no . . . actually, it was not the dark so much as it was the lions and tigers and bears which moved and prowled about on the wall above my bed!

Once, during a winter windstorm, those animals were so menacing that I flew out of that cold porch, raced into my parents' bedroom and landed squarely on top of my startled mother. I lost no time telling her about the big lions, tigers, and bears. To this day, I remember she did *not* tell me I was being silly. She did not remind me that our apartment was on the third floor and that it would be hard for the bears to get me. She didn't roll her eyes and suggest that I was a little girl with a big imagination (even though that was true!). She didn't send me back to bed by myself, nor did she threaten to shorten my life if I woke them again.

No, not at all. Calmly, she listened to me without interruption or making any comment, and I got the feeling she believed my panic. When I'd finished, she tucked me under the covers between her and my dad; and, somehow, I knew she understood my trembling fear and my story of the wild zoo on the sun porch.

Wise lady, that one, because I remember that after I'd calmed down, she whispered, "I'd like to show you something in your room. May I?" I wasn't too thrilled about leaving the warm coziness of my parents' bed, but I trusted her. Hand in hand, we went back to the sun porch; and, sure enough, the lions, tigers, and bears were still there—over the wall above my bed—moving, jumping, and just as scary as they had been before.

"Joyce, honey," my mother said softly without turning on the light, "look out the windows. Do you see the trees there? Now, look how the corner street lamp shines right through those bare tree branches." I looked.

"Well," she continued, "when the wind blows those branches, the light *behind* the trees makes those dancing shadows on this wall. Do you understand?" she asked gently. Then she brought her fingers together and made the shadow of a small animal's head on the wall, as I'd seen other adults do with the lights from a home movie projector to a screen, and I believed her. Those *were* shadows. But, I was thrilled because she believed me. She thought those moving shadows *looked* like wild animals, too.

So that I would be even more reassured, she found a small lamp, put it on the floor, and turned it on. Then, to my amazement, the wild animals *really* went away! Almost willingly, I climbed in under my covers. She kissed me and said, "Daddy and I will be in our room. Do you think you can get back to sleep? I hope so. But if you can't, you come and sleep with us."

My mother believed my fear, but did not minimize it. She did not deny my panic. Somehow, she let me know that it was perfectly understandable to be scared spitless! She also let me know she was there and, if I couldn't accept her explanations about the shadows, then I was to come to her. Most of all, it seems to me now, that all of her responses were geared toward saying: "I believe you. I love you. And I am going to try to change your circumstances, if I can. But I won't be too far away, leaving you to face your fears . . . so know that we are close and we'll take care of you."

Wesley didn't need to have someone pat him on the back and tell him he was silly and making too much of that barking dog. Neither do any of us. What we need is to have our feelings believed . . . and please, dear God . . . give us someone to listen who takes our fears seriously!

Number Three Response: *Tell Wesley what to do.*

Wesley's pleading voice and panic-stricken face begged for help. I could have assumed the role of problem-solver, put on my thinking cap, and launched into a combination of brilliant and boring solutions. I might have said something like this:

"Calm down, Wesley. I'll tell you what you should do. Here are my instructions:

"(1) You ride past that dog as fast as you can, and while you're going by him,

"(2) you sing at the top of your voice, and as loud as you can, because music hurts dogs' ears. And the last thing is this—

"(3) As you're riding your bike and singing, pray and ask God to close that dog's mouth and keep it closed like He did in the Bible for Daniel, in the lion's den."

This approach would have done a great deal for my ego, my need to spiritualize every event of life, and my sense of accomplishment; but I'm afraid it wouldn't have done a whole lot for Wesley. Needless to say, if he followed my little three-point formula as best he could, but the dog bit him anyway, I could always justify my words by saying Wesley didn't do it *exactly* as I told him, or he failed to pray the prayer about closing the lion's mouth with enough faith.

And, think on this a second . . . if Wesley *had* been bitten by the dog, I could have called his mother and reminded her rather smugly and indignantly that I *told* Wesley what to do. I could also jab her with the needle of, "And, had he done what I suggested, he would have been just fine!"

When we are in our unworld crisis, we often hear the prescriptions, the advice, and the spiritual admonitions of others from their well-insulated, second story windows. They tell us if we had listened to them, if we had read that book, if we had made that phone call, if we had just prayed with more faith, if we had been "into the Word" and having early morning devotions, if we had confessed and repented of our sins, if we had only . . . , if we had only . . . , and the list is endless.

I do not struggle with people who feel called by God (or whomever) to be Job's comforters and problem solvers. They are well meaning, perhaps even totally sincere. But I do feel sorry for people who seem to have a need to be an authority figure or have a Messiah complex; or, the person who believes they are wise with vast amounts of accumulated knowledge, and rich with the power of spiritual absolutes.

Those dogmatic problem solvers were very verbal while I was stumbling through the dark corridors of my unworld nightmare. Many times they spoke out of their ignorance rather than the truth, saying things like:

"I know your counselor is *not* a Christian because, if you were going to a Christian, you would not be seeking a divorce." (Wrong on two points: First, every counselor or pastor I saw—all six of them—were Christians. Second, I did not seek the divorce.)

Some softened the acrimony of their comments by saying, "Hey, Joyce, it's just a matter of bad timing on your part. You know, if you had just done so and so. . . ." There's no end of people telling you what to do and what not to do. To do even a tenth of what you are told, during an unworld crisis, would be impossible.

Other Christian leaders put on their high priest robes or their self-appointed prophets' hats and, with more than a little peevishness showing around their mouths, explained, "What you have to do, Joyce, is repent. Then I'll forgive you, for God and for others, but you must go back to your marriage and then you can continue your ministry." How dare any of us think, no matter who we are, that we have the power to be the priest of forgiveness for God! Another thing they did not know was that my forgiveness with God, about my marriage, was in excellent health; and also that sometimes, in a marriage, it's best not to exhume a dead body and try to resuscitate it back into a living and breathing corpse.

To have given Wesley my practical/impractical advice, or specially prepared formulas and fail-safe techniques, or even a quick, third grade course on religion and its benefits . . . the day his worst nightmare came true . . . may, just *may*, have helped him. But, I doubt it! On the other hand, God does seem to use whomever and whatever method He prefers, and well I know the folly of trying to second-guess God. So, I really don't know for sure if my words would have had any effect on Wesley or worked any healing for him.

But I know this: If I had tried to tell Wesley what he ought to feel, or how he should go about it; or, were I to recall my repeated success with this plan, and lecture him about how well it worked personally for me . . . and if, in the end, I had sent him off alone to face the big black barking dog of his nightmares, it would have been *absolutely criminally wrong* and *completely heartless* of me.

How easy it would have been to have stayed upstairs, safe and snug in my own well-insulated sanctuary, acting as if the dog was a simple problem, my solutional sermonizing obviously right, and my rationale for resolving the conflict as plain as the nose on Wesley's face. Or, I could have clucked my tongue with a "tsk, tsk" and boldly stated that the formula I'd outlined was clear and simple, and so workable that only a stupid person or a rebellious, disobedient sinner would miss the genius of my foolproof plan. I wonder where we ever got the idea that preachments and tactical oratory will do the trick and miraculously bring people's agonizing ordeals to closure?

I am all too familiar with another type of answer given to us when we are engulfed by the nightmare-come-true experience.

Number Four Response: *It's all your fault, Wesley!*

I guess from my own painful unworld experience and the unchristian comments from others, I believe (at least, for me) that the worst response of all to someone in the midst of their pain is this. For in our brokenness, we hear someone say, in a voice dripping with disgust and sarcasm:

"Wesley, you jerk! You brought this on yourself. It's all your fault.

"And, believe me, I knew this was going to happen. Someone told me the other day that you've made that dog mad every time you've ridden your bike down this road. I've heard the rumors that you've thrown rocks at him, taunted him, and teased him on your way home from school. Frankly, Wesley, if that's true, then you're just getting what you deserve! You've positively asked for this nightmare to come true!

"It wouldn't surprise me a bit if that old dog bites half your leg off! And if he does, the lesson will be good for you . . . because you gotta learn obedience. Yes sir, my boy, obedience is the name of the game. Now, you go ride that bike home and take your punishment like everybody else. And don't come back to me, cryin' and askin' for help!"

Ridiculing and scorning someone during their unworld predicament is bad enough, but I've discovered something else. Ranking right up there with our need to find and fix the blame on the guilty party is our sick, neurotic need to pronounce judgment and pass sentence on one another, based on insufficient evidence or hearsay.

In my unworld experience, I have run into this kind of rhetoric a great many times. I was emphatically told that surely I knew, if I agreed to a separation or considered a divorce, that I'd have to pay the consequences of such choices. "Didn't you?" they would ask. Some talked about my responsibility as a leader, others pontificated about my "willful" disobedience. Some pointed out that since I'd "made the bed" now I'd "have to lie in it." Still others pronounced me unforgivable and unusable; and certainly I've heard the world "disqualified" often enough.

As I thought through the range of emotions I felt at this time, some interesting pictures came to mind. Just think . . . if ever anyone could have been chastised, rebuked, and excommunicated from the church . . . told that they were unusable, unforgivable, and certainly disqualified to be a Christian leader or pastor . . . doesn't it strike you, that the apostle Peter would have won the biggest trophy of all time?

Who, more than Peter—a child of God, one of the chosen twelve—could have chosen a worse scenario than to deny he had any knowledge of Christ? Yet that was exactly what he chose to do. Repeatedly, not accidentally, Peter avowed— even cursed and swore—that he did not know, and had never known, anybody called Jesus. If ever a person disqualified himself for the ministry of the gospel, it was Peter.

Yet after Jesus' resurrection, out on a beach, we have one of the most remarkable conversations between Jesus and Peter ever recorded.

If you don't know the setting or the story, it's found in the twenty-first chapter of the book of John; and, basically, it goes like this:

A small group of Jesus' disciples—John, Peter, Thomas, Nathaniel, James, and a couple of others—went night fishing on the capricious sea of Galilee. By early dawn's light, they had caught nothing. Then as they looked toward the shore, they saw a man on the beach. . . . The stranger calls to them and asks the ancient question of all fishermen, "Did you catch any fish?"

When they tell him "No," to their surprise, this stranger proceeds to tell these seasoned fishermen to pull up their nets and put them down on the other side of the boat. Evidently, they felt they didn't have anything to lose, so they humored the stranger and did as they were told. Of course, they were astounded to find that their nets were so filled with fish that they couldn't draw them on board.

John finally recognizes the figure on the beach and says to Peter, "It's the Lord!" and the impulsive fisherman jumps out of the boat and swims to shore ahead of the others.

Jesus has a fire kindled with fish frying and some bread, by the time all the men gathered around and counted the biggest haul of fish they'd ever taken in. Jesus adds some more fish to the fire and invites them to eat breakfast with him there on the beach.

It is the conversation, after they have eaten, between Jesus and Peter, that touches me so deeply, and brings a special healing to my heart whenever I experience the awful un-world feelings of being unwanted, unusable, or particularly, the word: *disqualified*.

First, let me tell you what was *not* said. Actually, I wouldn't have been one bit surprised, based on some believer's inaccurate picture of God's character, to have read about this conversation and found that Jesus really nailed Peter to the wall with a powerful confrontation about the fisherman's triple denials. Or, perhaps Jesus could have lectured on how it appeared that Peter's denials were a spiritual and emotional betrayal in the style of one Judas Iscariot. At least, I might have expected Jesus to question Peter about his intent, his purpose, his guilt, his seeming lack of remorse; or, maybe I could have better understood, if Peter had taken a small shot at an apology to Jesus for his vehement denial. But no. . . .

The confrontation between Jesus and Peter that morning had no hint of any of those things. Jesus did not accuse Peter of disqualifying himself as a disciple or as a leader of God's kingdom. There wasn't even an implied message that Peter's calling to preach (his ordination papers or his preaching license) was being revoked. There was no threat of excommunicating Peter; and no rebuke, no slap on the wrist, and certainly Jesus never railed at the man about . . . "This is all your fault, Peter!" Jesus laid no guilt trips on Peter, nor did He expel him from service. No. None of that.

On the contrary, Jesus asks the same questions of Peter three times, and gives one directive. It seemed to me that the question Jesus asks Peter is a bottom line kind of question. Perhaps it's *THE* most important question of all our relationships because it asks, "Do you love me?"

After everything's been said and done in life, in our encounters with family, friends, and (especially) God, we want to know, above all else, "Am I loved?"

When Peter has answered yes to the question about loving Jesus, for the third time, then Jesus gives Peter the great mission statement, the great challenge, the great directive for Peter's life . . . saying, *"Peter, feed my sheep."*

I wonder what that must have felt like to be in Peter's wet tunic, trying to grasp that Jesus was not condemning, rebuking, or telling him to disappear for a few years, but actually promoting him . . . giving him an extraordinary calling to the ministry of the gospel. Think of it, Simon Peter, of whom

Jesus said, "And I tell you, you are Peter, and on this rock will I build my church and the powers of death shall not prevail against it."*

We must be comforted, you and I—who are hurting so with unworld feelings of being unusable, unable, and disqualified for service to our Lord. We must take hope in Jesus' words to Peter and understand, in God's eyes, that we are still valuable, usable, and richly qualified to fulfill our mission statement in the world around us.

Whether we are an eight-year-old Wesley, or a fifty-five-year-old Joyce, we must understand the emotional pain of unworld suffering. Even when our experiences are vastly different, still the pain of them is just as real, the fear just as terrifying to both of us. And we both need the comfort of *God's* approval.

As a believer in God, a follower of Christ, and one who calls herself a child of God . . . I have often wondered and thought about how our Lord expects me to respond, what He wants me to do, and when He wants me to act.

If Christ were physically here on earth today, I'd have no trouble imagining the way He might have handled Wesley's fears or how He might have addressed my pain.

I feel certain that the Lord *could* have given Wesley a thousand and one battle strategies, all guaranteed to outwit that dog; or, He *could* have worked a small, lesser-type miracle and turned the big black dog into a furry six-week old puppy, happily sunning himself by the side of the road; or (and Wesley would have *loved* this . . .) he could have made the dog evaporate entirely.

Also, Christ, being the great teacher, *could* have sat Wesley down, as he had done with more than 5,000 on the slopes and foothills, and preached His most eloquent and perfect, heal-

*Matthew 16:18, *Revised Standard Version.*

ing sermon. I'm sure Wesley, even though eight years old, would have understood the message. The Lord *could* have also become Wesley's just judge and fair jury, and there would have been no misjudging the circumstances.

But I think . . . as I read through and study the life of Christ, and as I see the truths He taught, both by the parables and stories He told, and the examples of His responses to various people throughout His ministry . . . I think Christ *would* have done one and only one thing for Wesley the day of the barking dog. I believe our Lord would have said,

Number Five Response: *I'll be right down, Wesley!*

Listening to the sheer panic in Wesley's voice, seeing the pale face, and reading the fear in his frightened eyes, I'd like to believe that not only our Lord, but any of God's children, would have quickly moved to be with Wesley. I remember telling Wesley I'd be right down and then just *racing* down the stairs.

After I hugged him, I said, "Wesley, it will be all right! Now you get on your bike and I'll walk beside you. I'll walk you all the way home."

"He's going to get me!" Wesley wailed. "It's my worst nightmare come true!" As I helped him pick up his bike, he kept insisting that his little life was all over.

"Wesley, listen to me. I'm going to walk right beside you, and if that dog comes after you, he's going to have to deal with me first!"

Wesley muttered without too much conviction, "Oh, sure," and he climbed on his bike.

"No, it's true," I said, raising my voice a little. "If he even gets *near* us, I'll tear off his legs. I'll beat him up. Believe me, he's going to get to *me* first and I'll crush his elbows!"

"Yeah," said Wesley. He hung his head, shaking it in disbelief, and reluctantly started peddling.

I walked down our driveway with one hand steadying his bike and we set out towards the road. Wesley was dramatically tragic. He looked as if he were a condemned man. And, sure enough, the dog was right there on the edge of the lot between the houses, barking his lungs out. Wesley still had no color at all in his face, but he kept his eyes fixed straight ahead.

Of course, the dog had no intention of ripping anybody apart. ("Good thinking, dog," I said mentally.) He was, as I figured, just a dog who delighted in barking because it seemed soothing to his throat, gave him a sense of importance, or something; but, most of all, perhaps the dog knew that barking upset little people rather well. You could tell the dog was having a fine time and was rather enjoying the whole scene.

Through his clenched teeth, and over the din of the noise, Wesley wailed, "He's gonna git me! I know it! It's my worst nightmare come true!" But we just kept going down the road toward his house.

After we were well past the dog who, incidentally, was still sitting in the same spot and still barking, I got a good look at Wesley's face. I was somewhat relieved. His color had returned to his cheeks and there seemed to be no residual of fear left around his eyes. I understood he had fully recovered and was in relatively fine shape when he abruptly instructed me to stop. Then, in very pleasant and courteous terms, he asked me to stay right where I was.

"What?" I blurted out. "Right here, almost in the middle of the road?" He nodded yes.

"For goodness sake, Wesley, why?"

He pointed down a little side road which veered off the main road to a neighbor's house and explained, "I want you to wait for me right here. I'm going to go down there and see if that lady will buy something from me. And then, when I get back, you can walk me home."

The boy has charm, because I stood right there and waited without saying "yes," "no," or "just a minute," as Wesley zipped off down the road and disappeared into the house.

I couldn't believe it. There I stood, in that stupid shorts outfit, feeling slightly mentally deranged . . . no makeup, my hair needing a perm, alone, and now, oh no, facing a growing stream of afternoon traffic. There were school buses, neighbors returning home from work, mothers chauffeuring their children or going to the store . . . however, there was nothing to do but wait for Wesley, idiotically smile, and wave my fingers in tentative hellos.

Give me credit—I was trying to find the humor in the situation. But we had just barely moved into the neighborhood. We were new, and I felt rather silly standing out there on the roadside. Besides that, I thought it was a terrible way to meet new people, especially one's neighbors. For a moment, I considered shouting to them, as they drove on by me, that I was a world-famous author disguised as a middle-aged lady hobo walking across America, gathering material for my newest book . . . but I lost my nerve because I figured one look at me and the evidence wouldn't be too convincing.

A few weeks after that unforgettable experience with Wesley—and yes, he did sell a "ton" of stuff to the other neighbor lady—it dawned on me that not only did no one stop and ask me what in the world I was doing out there, but to this day (months later) none of our neighbors have spoken to us. Perhaps they are trying to decide about the mental condition of the woman in the grubby shorts suit who had this ludicrous grin on her face and who waved as though she was the official welcome-wagon lady for the area. How would I know?

The memory of that afternoon is still warm and healing to my heart. I never saw Wesley again ... he and his parents moved away somewhere ... but I won't forget him.

I did choose to take the chemotherapy sessions ... I did experience mild to severe side effects. And whether or not I've been granted a remission, or mercifully been pronounced cured ... remains to be seen. At least, for now, I know the name of the malignancy; I've had a chance to see how I would absorb or throw off the disease; and I have seen the good and the terrible consequences and conclusions of my choices as they have wrought themselves on family and friends. And, from Wesley, I have gained some new perspectives into the many ways I can be responsive to others when their worst nightmare comes true and when they suffer their greatest un-world pain.

One Ray Of Hope

For I can never forget these awful years; always
my soul will live in utter shame.

*Yet there is one ray of hope: his compassion never
ends.* It is only the Lord's mercies that have
kept us from complete destruction.

Great is his faithfulness; his loving kindness
begins afresh each day.

My soul claims the Lord as my inheritance;
therefore I will hope in him.

Lamentations 3:20–24
The Living Bible

8

Moving out of the center of the storm of controversy, as part of my chemotherapy treatments, proved to be a much bigger task than I had imagined. I know that even moving across the street brings its own hazards so I hardly dared think about all the intricate details of starting my life over again. However, after the California house sold and the divorce was in process, I knew I'd have to pack up and leave everything I held near and dear.

I was counseled to get away from the storm for a few months (or for however long it took), and go into a restful exile somewhere. Especially since there was an abundance of painful pressures and stressful situations caused by the furor of my marital difficulties and the high visibility factor of my life.

So, I began seeking a rental place near the water, like a place on a small lake which would be soothing to the raw places of my soul. Hopefully I'd be able to recuperate, and I'd put some time and distance between myself and the raging outburst of public opinion. Surely, I reasoned, my critics would grow tired of their own rhetoric and would get on with the work and back to their lives. Color me BRIGHT NAIVE.

By the time I'd checked out several areas in California and two or three other states, for lakeshore rentals, I was very discouraged. Nothing seemed right. Also I think there is a vast difference between a person *choosing* to go on a sabbatical, or taking a leave of absence, and a person who is being banished and pressured by circumstances or other people to relocate and disappear. Our emotions can handle a sabbatical much better than a forced move to the backside of the desert of obscurity.

There was nothing but confusion in my mind as to what I should do, how I should work things out, or where I should go. Finally, through Francis Heatherley and a friend, Diana Thomas, I learned of a Swiss Chalet–type cabin in Texas owned by Karen and Mark Wiggins.

The cabin, set back off a winding dirt road, was almost hidden in a tiny forest of cedar and yaupon trees. It was made of blue-gray stained cedar siding, with large windows and spacious decking, and was surrounded on three sides by a small tranquil Texas lake. And fortunately the rent was only $250 a month. In retrospect, it should be said that probably there is no place where one can go to dodge or escape the unworld's wounding. But there was no way to understand this then.

Texas, that summer, was its typical hot and humid self. But after I got moved, my children and the few friends who saw my new-to-me little cabin, pronounced it "Perfect!" Meaning, "It's God's place for you to heal."

I felt raw, torn, and hemorrhaging. But, somehow the right thing to do seemed to be that I should try, no matter how hard it was, to tackle the overwhelming task of putting my mind and soul back together again. Somewhere inside of me there was a faint, almost imperceptible voice that whispered, "You mustn't give up." On the kitchen wall was a framed plaque from a friend who was terminally ill with cancer, which read,

Endings
must come before
new
beginnings.

So, I made an attempt to stay alive each day.

The cabin was well chosen, actually a gift from the Wiggins family and God . . . rather like an intensive care unit set up in an unlikely place, on the edges of a lake. However, it was in Texas, beside those calm and peaceful waters of Lake Mexia, that I was dismayed by the contrast between my surroundings and the violent turbulence going on within me.

I came to grips with the unsettling fact that I'd lost almost all of the personal friends I ever had. This reality slammed vehemently into my conscious mind. I began to understand that some friends, particularly those who had been long-time friends and very supportive to me during the ten years of physical pain with TMJ, were totally insensitive to my comments and explanations about my present emotional pain. It was as though, when my pain was purely physical, they had been able to accept and deal with it, but they regarded the trauma which surrounded the breakup of my marriage as a contagious disease. Who could blame them, really? I couldn't, because I suffered from the same kind of denial about Christian marriages in trouble . . . sort of an attitude which said, "Look the other way, hide it, and God will just take care of it all."

Most painful to me, however, was my friends' willingness to believe what others said (or surmised) about my separation or my reasons for wanting to leave California.

Baffling, too, were the various responses from family members. A few were wonderfully supportive and never changed that support. Others were warm to me, then cool, and finally silent. Still others let me know, at some point, that they could not, or would not, deal with me and my situation.

Always, whether it was family or friends, the very ones I just *knew* would love and care for me were the exact ones who left as quickly as possible. Some of those dearest to me, long time friends, relatives, and associates who left my life three years ago, have stayed away and have never spoken another word to me.

I was saddened and disappointed with Christian organizations and some Protestant denominations that brag, as it were, about their ministry, interest, and support of the Christian family when none of them made contact or reached out to my "family," my children. Apparently, no one guessed that Laurie and Rick, with their own young families, were in deep pain and needed some loving support.

Unworld people experience their ordeal and then are shocked and stunned by the loss of friends, family, and associates. There we stand, almost totally alone; and, at precisely the time of our greatest need for family and friends . . . we feel abandoned. We wonder where the support groups are for us. We've heard of organizations and support groups for almost every other tragic situation . . . why not for us? Christians go first to church to find help and care; but, if we go and are rebuked or rejected, then where do we go and who can we find? We want to stand on some street corner and scream, "Won't somebody stop, speak, and surround us with some kind of nourishing understanding?"

The unworld tearing process seems to break down the very inner fibers of our spirit. It saps and drains us of strength or energy. Daily we encounter a new and unexpected crisis. We stumble about in a dense emotional fog and we are stunned with the unfairness of life and its unabated stream of losses. We cringe with the ever present fear that this new loss or the next blow will be the one to finish off the annihilation process.

What's more, while losing friends and family you add your own paranoid thoughts and everyday craziness. Part of the daily struggle you face is the ridiculous fact that it is routinely impossible to remember even the most simple things you've done all you life. You feel positively stupid when you forget *everything*.

"Oh, dear, *now* where have I left my car keys?"

"Why am I here at the store . . . did I want apples or milk?"

"Officer, no I didn't know I was exceeding the speed limit. I'm going through a divorce. Have you ever been divorced? Well, sir, I don't remember where I started, where I've been, or how I got to this place on the road."

The absurd things you forget eventually bring you to ask the terribly serious question, "Oh, dear God, just who am I?" Everything, including time, dates, things, places, and people all seem to blur and blend into each other . . . melting into one giant memory loss. You don't know where you are or what you are supposed to be doing most of the time and frankly, Scarlet, you just don't very much care.

For me, that summer at Lake Mexia, I responded to life as though I was someone in the deepest throes of the bereavement process. If you have ever lost someone close to you, do you remember the "six-weeks-after-the-death" period? The funeral is over, your family has returned to their own homes, you've written thank you notes for the flowers and the casseroles which were sent, and now the finality of it all settles in. Reality forces itself into your consciousness and slams into your soul with a terrible velocity; and you know, you absolutely know, your loved one is *not* away on a business or pleasure trip. He or she is not in a hospital or living in a distant city or foreign country. You know that loved one will never come home, will never hold you, will never talk to you, will never, never, never *be again*—here on this earth. He is dead. She is dead. Gone . . . and life, as you once knew it, will never be again. Heaven? Oh, yes . . . but here? No.

The summer of my grief the depressing, overwhelming sense of unbearable losses and inconsolable grief never left me, not even for an hour, that whole time. I am alive now, and owe a huge debt of gratitude to those *dear few* who tried to keep me carefully wrapped in a cocoon of love so I wouldn't self-destruct. Yet, living was like being in a semicoma condition. Hearing but not hearing. Seeing but not seeing. Being but not being. I wasn't able to take everything on a "one day at a time" basis . . . it was more like trying to survive one hour to the next, and sometimes from one minute to the next.

Summer sweltered itself away and finally all of Texas slipped into September. My children and a couple of friends ended their visits with me and returned to their own homes. It was then, when things grew very quiet and peaceful, that I took a mental inventory of my life. I felt I'd get a better grip on some inner healing. The pain eased a little bit, and I was somewhat revived. (Not much, you understand, but enough to feel, a few moments at a time, a little more like myself.) It was as though, on some days, my vision cleared and I was able to see. The cabin, the lake, the people, and some present and future realities came into sharper focus.

Before I knew it, I was experiencing the fall season. By the time autumn was fully upon the lake, the leaves in the forest that surrounded my cabin began to lose their deep green shades and turned pale with lovely subdued colors. They never burst into those brilliant New England reds and bright vibrant yellows, but they were magnificent in their own soft-spoken way. It was as if God planned for the soft colors of the leaves to soothe and quietly heal my spirit.

The beauty of autumn's faded collage of colors and shapes blended in with the blue-gray siding of the cabin. Some days the landscaping and the colors made me feel as if I were living in a misty French watercolor painting. Even the graceful blue herons, white egrets, and early arriving winter ducks brought beauty to my barrenness.

Each day I would see a little more of God's creation and hear a little more of God's song. On some days, however, I'd open the mail or answer the phone and suddenly—without warning—dark pain would strike and close in on me again. It would completely seal off my soul from all sights and sounds. The emotional pain of my losses screamed so loudly that I'd find myself deaf and blind once more. The soundless gloom of those days still frightens me.

The day in autumn that I *do* remember, and will probably never forget, was one when Karen Wiggins, for some reason, stopped by. It may have been the day she brought a vegetable offering from her wonderful garden; an invitation to dinner with them in their magnificent country home; a plant in a basket; or some beautiful pieces of fresh salmon. Or, she just may have made the visit to "check" on me . . . I can't recall.

As I walked Karen out to her car that day, and was about to say good-bye, I realized there seemed to be something special about the moment, as if I was about to experience one of those rare mini-healing moments. Bandages seemed to loosen up from over my eyes and it was as though plugs were removed from my ears. I experienced a slight but perceptible burst of new strength. It was only a tiny and fragile feeling of aliveness, but some of the dreaded pall of depression which so stunned my senses seemed to lift. It felt *wonderful*.

Karen's sweet grace and regal beauty, combined with the scenic grandeur of outdoors, was awesome. I looked about the forest and the clearing around the cabin. Drinking in the marvelous fall sight, I breathed aloud, to her, "Ah, Karen, this place is really so beautiful! I know I'm *supposed* to be here and," I added optimistically, "I feel certain I'm going to heal here . . . maybe I'll even be able to hear the music again."

Karen smiled, nodded her head affirmatively, and then casually she answered—in a voice warmed by her soft Texas drawl—"Oh, but just *wait until spring!*"

I doubt that I will ever forget Karen, her words, or the cup of hope she held out for me. The sentence, brief as it was, held more promise in it than I had allowed myself to dare think or dream. For a second or two my heart beat quite irregularly, and then it resumed its normal rhythm. I hardly remember if Karen and I talked of anything else because I was so caught up in the enheartening word *spring*. As I waved and watched her back her car out of the gravel-covered, tree-arched drive-way, I began to ponder the meaning and ramifications of her words . . . *wait for spring*.

Perhaps this is the point where you, the reader, are presently in the midst of your unworld hell, and you're thinking, "Nice for you, lady! Listen, I'd kill to have a cabin on the lake for a quiet time of healing! I'd give anything to leave my place and go somewhere beautiful and escape my problems." I don't blame you, if this is what you're thinking. I would have thought it too—had I not lived the eye-opening reality.

It is very true that when we move we take our problems with us. Another house, another new state, another apartment, another job, another car, another nursing home, another set of circumstances do not change the basic elements of our problems, our pain, or our hurts. We take joy *and* sorrow with us. We take the big and the small struggles as well as the pleasurable and wonderful memories with us. In short, moving *from* something won't work at solving the hard problems of our lives. Moving *to* something and knowing that we cannot deny the enigma of our trouble is a very different thing.

Karen had, in a few words, painted a picture of hope for me, in her loving call for me to stay around, to "wait for spring." What I didn't fully realize at the time was that my quaint and charming cabin on the lake would become both a place of beauty and a place of facing and dealing with some stark realities.

I wondered if the winter's chill would ever lift. Or would I freeze to death because of others' icy rejection? Would people, or those in Christian leadership, never stop their endless judgments, critical remarks, and barrage of untruthful attacks? I wondered, if spring did come, would I be through the darkest part of my recovery . . . or, would it never end? Was the beauty and serenity of the lake cabin a very deceptive beauty? These and other questions haunted me. We never can be assured that moving will be our answer. Sometimes when we solve one problem we get a new set. The cabin on the lake brought that truth home to me.

I didn't know, for instance, that during one heavy rainstorm the placid shimmering lake would rise four feet above its banks, bringing two feet of black, muddy, swirling water into my cabin which stopped just an inch under my piano keyboard.

Furthermore, I wasn't prepared for the huge Texas-sized roaches which infested the cabin and came to stay. And, because of my lifetime fear (possibly phobia) of snakes, I was not able to accept the water moccasins which terrorized me. Especially the one in my shower or the other one behind the bathroom door. So, with these menacing encounters and my fragmented emotions, I had grave doubts about being able to wait for anything, much less for spring. The losses were too great, the fears too overwhelming, and the emotional damage too comprehensive.

If spring came, would it mean that I'd withstand all the malicious and untrue things being spread about me? Would I be able to say to myself, "It's all right. Accept this as unfair. Life, after all, *is* unfair. Don't let this all get to me or hurt me." I didn't know if I was that strong or not.

If spring came, would I have anything to say about the treacherous turns in the path of my unworld journey? Would I ever be well enough to write and pour myself out on my yellow-lined tablets? Would I be able to go back to reading three or four books at a time? Would I be able to concentrate on printed words for more than two minutes (or two lines) at a time? And, by spring, I wondered, what would I have learned about God and people? Anything? Or, did it even matter?

I wish I could write that because of the scenic beauty of

my surroundings, or because God came down and worked an absolute miracle every morning at 9:00 A.M., healing came to me within a few months—just in time for spring. But that was not the case.

Actually, as a woman suffering from the unworld encounter, I was *not* able to be courageous. I could *not* say that the angry, judgmental words spoken or written about me didn't hurt. Frankly, they destroyed and devastated me. Furthermore, I could not pray . . . not even a little bit. Nor did I have the ability to read. The words wouldn't connect or make sense, and that knowledge was unthinkable to me. I had *always* read.

I was unable to stop the constant flow of tears. I cried all the time. I couldn't trust myself even when I went into town to the grocery store because I never knew when an incident or a passing thought would set me off and I'd just stand there like some idiot, sobbing. Tears would come when I expected them, and when I didn't.

I found I could sit at the piano for hours, touching the keys, but only occasionally could I make my rigid fingers play. Most of the time, my vocal chords would not open and close properly, so I didn't sing too much. It was a puzzling enigma because I had played the piano and sung for most of my entire life. I would simply sit there and cry.

I despaired that regardless of the time spent in the cabin, neither time nor God would ever bring a spring. Never could I have foreseen the wild mix of emotional feelings I'd experience, or the intensity of people's cruelty, in the months between that fall and spring.

How do we begin to heal from our unworld experiences? I do not know about you . . . I don't know all the "facts" about your ordeal, your crisis, or your severe pain. Even if I did, I would be unable to tell you, in detail, what you must do now. But, I do know what happened in my life. I may not be able to give you a detailed plan, an explicit scenario, or a 400-page script to follow. Nor do I want to. But, I can walk you through my wait for spring. Perhaps my attempt in sharing will bring some meaningful wholeness, in some way, to your brokenness.

The most healing route to my recovery began with God and His grace, and continued on with caring humans. The key equation for bringing about wholeness in anyone's life is the combination of God and people working together. At least it was, and continues to be, for me.

Let me tell you about God first. I began sensing God's presence in the cabin during that fall ... but only in brief flashes and fleeting moments. It might be impressive to you, if I could say that I read my Bible, prayed, and had my quiet meditations and devotions every morning, but that simply was not true. Most of the time, I stumbled numbly through my days. I struggled with the simplest of chores, tried desperately to remember things, and fell into bed exhausted and weary but was unable to sleep more than what felt like a few minutes at the most.

Not too many weeks after I finished painting the kitchen area, and was a little more settled into the cabin, an incident occurred which made me smile, and took me straight back a hundred years to my upbringing as the daughter of an evangelical minister.

I recalled many a church service, prayer meeting, or Bible study group where a person from Dad's congregation stood up, told of being in the midst of some terrible conflict and how they were having to make a crossroads choice or decision. They'd go on, relating how they had reached for their Bible, prayed that God would give them an explicit answer, and then they had just let the Bible fall open at random. Sure enough! "Whatta ya know?" There, on that very page, was God's divine solution. It was sort of a biblical roulette, a game which they always won.

That kind of testimonial which said, "The Bible fell open

and behold . . . " was very popular in my childhood, and probably still is now, as it implies (1) I am using and reading God's Word (I'm so spiritual); (2) I can pick just about any verse and make it apply and translate into the solution (no sweat); and (3) it practically shouts that God himself has personalized His divine message for me (yeah, I got God's approval and blessing).

This very fond memory of my earlier days came graphically back to me one morning, in the cabin, as I was absent-mindedly dusting a small end table. I was not thinking, looking for answers, or praying . . . actually the gears of my mind were somewhere between numb and neutral. But, as I moved my Bible to one side it slipped through my fingers, fell, and . . . guess what? It landed on the floor, wide open to the book of Romans, in the New Testament.

Now I am not going to claim that God came down, opened His book, and *red-lined* the part He wanted me to read. But, neither will I ever believe that the Bible just opened to Romans for some accidental reason or was merely a semi-remarkable coincidence. Consider my desperate need. I was a broken child of God. I trust you'll see in the next few pages that no matter what the origin or manner of this incident, it was a most strategic and meaningful bridge between my Maker and me.

My powers of concentration were limited, at best, that day—as they often are during unworld ordeals—and I didn't have too much ability to absorb the sentences or paragraphs; but, my eyes did catch the verses at the end of chapter eight.

The glimpse I got, at first, was subliminal advertising at its very best. In that brief moment (as I now can look back and comprehend), I took my first infinitesimally small steps toward a powerful truth about God's basic character.

A blurry idea began forming in my mind, and breaking

through my memory was the realization that Romans 8 ended with an astounding pronouncement.

Read the apostle Paul's words for yourself:

> Who shall separate us from the love of Christ? Shall tribulation, or distress, or persecution, or famine, or nakedness, or peril, or sword?
>
> As it is written, For thy sake we are killed all the day long; we are accounted as sheep for the slaughter.
>
> Nay, in all these things we are more than conquerors through him that loved us.
>
> For I am persuaded, that neither death, nor life, nor angels, nor principalities, nor powers, nor things present, nor things to come,
>
> Nor height, nor depth, nor any other creature shall be able to separate us from the love of God, which is in Christ Jesus our Lord.*

The truth of this message fragrantly floated across my mind, offering just a whiff of hope. For I remembered that the eighth chapter ends by unequivocally declaring that *nothing separates us from the love of God.*

Nothing? No. Absolutely nothing! Then, I caught my mind regressing a bit. "Come on, wait a minute here!" I told myself. Why is this familiar passage of scripture having such an impact on me? Haven't I been taught from childhood the old truth that God loves me? I questioned. Haven't I sung "Jesus loves me, this I know, for the Bible tells me so"? What's my problem, then? It seemed too simplistic of a well-known truth for me to really apply to the intensity of my brokenness.

Nevertheless, from that time forward, I watched as my awe, trust, love, and respect for God's character and His divine and unconditional love rose to some new heights within me!

---

*Romans 8:35–39, *King James Version*.

I also had to deal with another closely related issue. While God affirmed His love and assured me through His Word that nothing separated me from that great and glorious love . . . I had to understand that I could not expect, nor should I expect, the same responses from all of His children. It was impossible to ignore the fact that many of my brothers and sisters in the faith had taken a *very* different approach with me about "what" or "who" separated me from God.

On one hand, Christian leadership (in particular) told me, during my marital separation, they loved me. Most assured me of God's love, and even of their daily prayers. More often than not, people offered their secret and private friendship. I had to face the painful reality that while most all of my peers and leadership agreed that nothing separated me theologically from God's love or theirs . . . their response to me was to *treat* me as if my particular "circumstances" did indeed separate me from God's love and theirs. In essence, I regularly heard, "Joyce, God loves you and I love you." That sentence was followed with words like *But* and *However*. Their love was far from unconditional . . . and constantly qualified and defined.

Those comments, as painful as they were for me to hear, especially when it really hit me that people were saying "I love you privately but . . . " helped me to learn a lesson or two about my own response to others. Also, conditional love versus unconditional love brought up some new thought in me.

It seemed, after talking with thousands of hurting Christians, and after going through my own excruciating unworld experiences: No one's love, save God's love alone, can be described as unconditional. I believe we can try to love others in the very best way we can but that it is not possible for us, as humans, to love unconditionally. That's God's divine method of loving.

For years I have felt that in a few relationships with dear

loved ones that I *did* love them (as close as I could) with God's type of unconditional love . . . but I believe now that was not the case. Our human love, even to those closest and dearest to us, has some fixed qualifiers, various built-in conditions which we insist need to be met; or the love we give has some threads, strings, ropes, even chains attached to it. We like to call our love unconditional, but it isn't that at all.

Is it any wonder that after all the assorted disclaimers and the multiple qualifiers we and others attach to "God loves you and so do I, *but* . . . " that my mind (and yours) would boggle a bit over the utter simplicity and yet grandeur of Paul's words, in Romans, about God's unique and classic love?

That day, in the cabin, I moved my Bible from the end table to the music rack on the piano; and from then on, until I moved away, I kept it there, opened to that passage of scripture. I doubt that I missed a day of sitting on that piano bench and pouring what little concentration I had into the eighth chapter of Romans.

I read it over and over again. I read it through my tears and through my hurt and anger. I read it when none of the words made sense. I read it when I understood only parts of it. I read it when I doubted . . . or questioned its veracity, and I read it even when I couldn't comprehend how God would somehow *still* love me.

Once after telling my cousin, Mary Ellen, about those last verses in Romans 8, she embroidered and framed a beautiful stitchery which personalized the verse and said,

> Nothing
> can separate you,
> Joyce,
> from the love of God
> which is in Christ Jesus the Lord.
> *Romans 8:35, 39*

I hung this new treasure next to my bathroom mirror so I'd be sure and see it every day. Later she sent a second stitchery reminder with Psalms 57:1, 2, to give me hope.

I remember just sort of plodding through those long days and the even longer nights. As I said, I barely played the piano or sang but I did keep reading and pondering the unbelievable words of Romans 8.

Then, on one of those nameless days, my memory reminded me that, years before, an author, my friend Ruth Harms Calkin, had sent me her personal thoughts about that very passage in Romans. Frantically I searched through my files and notebooks and I finally managed to locate her letter, in a box which I'd put into a rented storage unit. I took Ruth's typewritten page to the cabin, placed it on the piano next to my open bible and, along with a songbook of Dan Burgess's called *Press On*, I read all three things almost every day, all through the fall and winter months.

Ruth's words vividly described all the awful and hideous things which *could* or *might* convince her that God no longer loved her. The list included most of the truly fearful unworld realities I've ever experienced or read about in my mail. But, Ruth ended this heart-moving piece by stating, "None of these things, or all of them heaped together, can budge the fact

That I am dearly loved
Completely forgiven
And forever His
Through Jesus Christ
God's beloved son!"

Many times, after I'd read Romans 8 and Ruth's words, then I'd take one finger and trace the melody of one of Dan's songs on the piano. There was the one called "In God's Time," and of course the lead song, "Press On." But, most touching of all, to me, was one entitled "You Are There." The lyrics were based on the magnificent 139th Psalm where David begins with the words, "O Lord, you have examined my heart and know everything about me. You know when I sit or stand. When far away you know my every thought. You chart the path ahead of me, and tell me where to stop and rest. . . . "*

The chorus in Dan's song, "You Are There," reads,

I can never be lost to Your spirit,
I can never get away from Your love,
If I go up to the heavens
   or descend to the earth below
You are there
You are there!

If I ride the winds of morning to the ocean
Even there Your hand will guide and strengthen me.
If I try to hide in darkness
Still Your light shines through
And You're there.
You are there,
You are there!

Even this moment, as I write these pages, Dan's songbook is on the table in front of my desk, and still . . . it brings tears to my eyes with the remembrance of how the music and lyrics were like a warm, soothing balm to the raw places inside me.

I know, during those tumultuous days, I was kept alive by God's truth in the Romans passage of scripture and by some of God's choicest children!

Ruth's words, Dan's music, Karen Wiggins's and Diana Thomas's friendship, each week a phone call from Clare Bauer and a few people like Anita Donaldson who came to my rescue during the long months of my critically grave condition in the intensive care cabin by the lake, saved my life.

---

*Psalm 139:1–3, *The Living Bible.*

I've already told about Karen and Mark Wiggins. They continued their gentle and uninterrupted schedule of supportive caring. They came into my life during those awful days and always seemed to bring a calming peace into the vortex of my stormy unworld battles.

Also, I grew immensely fond of my beautiful neighbors—Mr. Tacker, up the road, and Mrs. Lindley, beyond the trees the other way. Consistently they treated me with a mix of God and Texas love. I will never forget the role they unknowingly played in simply bringing down to earth balance into my days. They, with their sweet attitudes and tiny kindnesses, provided some dearly needed normalcy which I know helped me keep from going totally insane.

Last, but positively not least, in my struggle to survive the holocaust of those early months at the cabin, was one man—Francis Heatherley. And although he had made a number of crucial choices and had chosen to make significant changes in his life, and was, at that time, encountering the main fury of his own unworld hell . . . still Francis became a one-person support group to me.

Many times he drove out to the cabin to take care of me. Often he went straight to the Post Office in Mexia, picked up the volumes of mail I was receiving (roughly 500 to 600 letters a month) and brought it out to the cabin. He spent hours reading almost every letter aloud to me. Francis (or "Doc," as so many call him) understood that I had little or no ability to concentrate, no self-confidence, no strength to see any future, and no sense of purpose or mission. It is to Francis's immense credit, that even though he was terribly broken and suffering himself, he resolved to keep me spiritually and emotionally alive.

The mail provided the lifeline to both of us in our unworld anguish. Francis read those loving missives from grass roots people, real people, well people, hurting people, caring people, all the brothers-and-sisters-in-Christ people; and the letters came from every state in America and from all around the world.

The messages were astounding! Less than one-half of one percent of the mail was critical. The rest was overwhelmingly positive and supportive. These people filled each letter with their love in every conceivable manner. And many times, while reading someone's loving, healing words, we would be so deeply moved that Francis, unable to read because of his tears, would lay the letter aside . . . and we'd weep together.

During that time, while we were both suffering, the very special friendship we had enjoyed in our professional lives of publishing and ministry in past years took on deeper meaning. We found ourselves responding to a most beautiful love. A love which grew, pledged and committed itself to us in those dreadful agonizing months.

It was a love borne out of long-standing pain, but one that began to restore our individual wholeness and forged us into one. I cannot put my finger on the exact moment when our friendship love moved into a romantic love . . . only that it did. And since neither of us planned love's course, or for all the years we'd worked together foresaw it coming, we are today still surprised. We didn't dream God had such an unexpected gift for us. Especially that gift of love, given at the most unlikely, unbelievable time of our lives.

What I do know, of those times, was that God's hand shaped and provided for Francis and me an undeniable blending and fusion of His Word and His children. The Bible and the Romans 8 passage, the personal reflections by Ruth Calkin on the same chapter's ending, Dan Burgess's music, Mark and Karen Wiggins, my family and friends and cabin neighbors, turned out to be not only life saving for us, but one of the most relevant and important teachings of my life.

I can't say I fully saw those lessons or understood too

much of them while it was happening, but given these past two years to reflect on the process—I can see God's intricate tapestry. Especially clear was what I was learning about dealing with relationships. I am still marveling about what happens when there is a synthesizing between God and people, especially when the healing process is directed toward bringing wholeness to a wounded unworld person. The degree of emotional restoration which takes place is as powerful as it is awesome!

However, back then, I was still very broken, and there were many days and weeks out of those fall and winter months that I was unmistakenly alone, feeling cut off from the rest of the world, and yet with no desire or strength to join anyone . . . to go out into that world. The pressure and mix of rejection and criticism was still strong and so *on*going that it robbed me of the ability to see or to completely appreciate the loving efforts of God and the few people I did manage to be with.

Over and over, during that first autumn in the cabin, I pondered the theology of Romans 8. It seemed to me, even in spite of my limited mental and emotional skills, that Paul was trying his dead level best to emphasize—in neon-lit italics, as it were—the importance of understanding his message. There is a passionate sense of urgency when he assures us that nothing we think or imagine, nothing which prevails against us, and nothing we do separates us from the unconditional love of God. Oh, dear unworld person . . . what a thought!

Slowly (or as quickly) as I was able to absorb these wondrous words, I began to crystallize some clear truths about my own actions, decisions, and choices without having those thoughts colored by the words of my critics.

The knowledge began to seep and permeate, as it were, past my barriers and my own denial into the depths of my being. Was it possible that there was *not a thing* . . . not even my decision to file for legal separation, not the divorce itself, and not even the ugly statements and rumors about my relationship with Francis which others were hurling at me . . . that could come between God and me?

The truth was: *Nothing*, not even those things (both the true and the untrue), could shake God's love. Nothing could shock God. He knew all the facts. He knew my status with Him regarding sin and forgiveness. He knew the intent of my heart. Nothing could put a barrier between God and me. Each day God's beautiful words in Romans, and His ministering children in Mexia breathed the breath of wholeness into my crumbled life.

Later, that winter, before I had a chance to think much about the coming of spring's greenery and blossoms, I recalled Fredrick Buechner's book. I remembered my own writing which his book spawned while I was still back in California. I recalled the words I'd written about being sent to the room called rejection. The memory stirred a strange yet special comparison in my mind.

Here I was, slightly recovered, but still exposed to the continuing onslaught of rejection and criticism. Yet I could feel myself going into a brand new room. I'd say it was a strange feeling because I felt no threat, no hurt . . . only a sense that the room was a very sheltered place. It was a special feeling because I was not being pushed or sent through its doorway. Rather, I was being gently and carefully drawn into this newest of rooms. At the entrance I breathed a sigh of relief and took my first step across the threshold into the room called grace.

"Warm," "beautiful," and "protected" are the words which best describe the interior of the room. It was a spacious, airy refuge, and was lit by the sun streaming through the windows lining the walls.

The presence of God, like a rare perfume, wafted around

me stirring memories of the time my father drove us down a road in the middle of an orange grove on our first trip to Florida. The memory of orange blossoms was not unlike the delicately sweet scent of God's presence in this room called grace.

While I was still just inside the entrance, anticipating its beauty and breathing deeply of its original rich perfume, I nevertheless hung back a bit. Many people had made me feel I was unworthy, unfit, and unqualified as a wife, a mother, and as a woman. The question rose within me as to whether I could or should be allowed access to this unmistakable sanctuary named grace.

Whatever my peers, publishers, and Christian leadership people in general had hoped to accomplish with me by their hateful letters, pseudo-friendly phone calls, cancellations of my work or my speaking engagements, or their pregnant silences, they had achieved beyond their wildest dreams. I had been thoroughly intimidated by them, and I really did believe I was unworthy, unfit, and unqualified to work for God. Much less to stand in the same room with Him. So this newly discovered room called grace left me more than a little uneasy. "Do I deserve to be here?" I wondered.

My critics were all Christian people, God's children. Yet they were the very people who, while offering me their theoretical love, at the same time pronounced me sinful, unremorseful, and, in effect, separated from God. I came dangerously close to believing the lie.

In my mind's eye, I could see them outside the door, lining the hallway, shaking their heads in amazement as I made my way further into the room called grace.

However, in spite of my edginess, I did understand and believe God about Romans 8 and "nothing separating us," and I was experiencing the caring support from a few of God's children; so I decided to lighten up a bit and relax. After all, maybe (just maybe) in this wonderful and holy room called grace, I could even begin to trust God *and* His people!

I've known since I was a little girl about God's *saving* grace. It's that wonderful "amazing grace" which John Newton wrote about in one of our most famous and time-honored hymns. But I felt that what was happening in this room was not the saving kind of grace, but something else. A grace that was somehow very different. In fact, not a saving grace but rather a *sustaining* grace. A grace that was ongoing. A grace which continued to maintain, nourish, nurture, even cherish us. A grace to grow on. A grace which would vindicate us in the presence of our enemies. A grace which daily would authenticate our right standing with God. An unending grace strong enough to endure our worst unworld day and our most unpredictable tomorrows.

Only God could have thought up these two special graces—both so different, but both so equally needed and important! Never had I ever longed for, or needed, the sustaining grace of God more than in those early months at the cabin. Yet, at the same time, I think I never felt more unworthy to stand in that incredible room called grace and be so close to the awesome presence of God.

I cannot speak for anyone else who stands in the room called grace (and there are millions of us), but it seemed to me that each day in that room brought my life into sharper focus.

It was as if, with one hand, I mentally clung tenaciously to the truth of Romans 8. But my other hand was being held by the most choice children of God. Somehow I was enabled to reach out and grab the facts of my soul and my unworld ordeal in a realistic way and begin to really deal with them.

A new conviction began forming within me. I could see I was moving towards a significant encounter with God but, because the thought of it was not threatening or alarming to me, I was not defensive. Instead, I became determined to move straight ahead to the meeting. I almost welcomed it. Instinctively, I felt that this conversation with God would be the biggest single factor in setting my crushed life in order. (I know now, I got that right!)

Gradually, in the room called grace, as I reviewed the past circumstances of my life and the present events which were taking place, I was gently led to the position of baring my soul before God.

How beautiful that, in the privacy and intimacy of that astounding room called grace, God heard my anguished cry. What happened between us, in those holiest of holy moments, is still that ... *between us.* I will never be the same again. What's more, that special encounter with God can never be taken away from me. No person can belittle it. God will never forget that He granted His forgiveness. Nor will He ever remember my sins against me. It is enough to say that my past sins, failures, mistakes, and even the weakest traits of my character were left in God's capable hands that day!

I am aware that there will be some people, whether they are in leadership or in the church body, who will insist on hearing extra details, want more explanations, answers, and specific descriptions, and who will demand a more lengthy public statement from me (or from anyone who is a highly visible person). But, the important thing here is for us to bring the dark issues, the sins, the failures ... everything to God. I am not saying that there is no need to seek forgiveness from other people ... only that first, I believe, our right standing has to start with God and *His* forgiveness.

Also, I'm cognizant of the many times I have heard a Christian say, of another Christian, "You know, I just don't have much respect for so-and-so, because I haven't seen any sign of repentance."

I've known, too, of individuals who have been rejected by a whole congregation of people because the pastor (or some other authority figure) has said publicly and/or privately,

"During my talk with him (or her) I *saw* no remorse."

I have no idea how many times this was said of me . . . or who, exactly, said it. But, this I *do* know: No matter *who* we are, or what others think, say, or see about our standing with God, our repentance, or our heart-felt remorse—God's forgiveness, and God's merciful work of restoration in our lives are God's and our concern alone!

It is not fitting or right for a person to judge anyone on *any* basis . . . especially on whether or not we see "signs of remorse." We humans are unequivocally unqualified to even hazard a guess at someone's right or wrong position with God, much less make a judgment.

You and I, who have sinned (and I'm talking serious majority here!), can take comfort in the fact that precisely *because* God knows each and every dreadful detail about our sin . . . He does not turn from us. He does not abandon us or withhold His forgiveness. Believe me.

And I know, from experience, once we walk into the room called grace we find that God is waiting for us! He waits eagerly and lovingly to bring His unlimited forgiveness and His unconditional love into the panic and the pain of our terrified souls.

Once the fountain of God's forgiveness began to cascade over my parched soul, I was able to grasp an old but forgotten concept. I saw the timeless admonition about *trusting God* from a new and different angle. Perhaps this is nothing new to you—but, for me, the room called grace provided an eye-opening experience. The concept that came through, like a brilliant sunrise, was that I could trust God fully without fear or any reservations.

I could trust, unreservedly, God's entire character, His makeup, His divine intent for me, and His whole plans for mankind.

Think of this—we *can* trust God!

- God's *judgment* can be trusted because as our creator He alone knows all the facts and circumstances of our lives, our thoughts, and our emotions.
- God's *forgiveness* can be trusted because He has the unique authority to forgive us our sins and, once forgiveness is given, He has the unique ability to lose His memory of those sins.
- God's *mercy* can be trusted because He understands the complexities of our souls, minds, and lives so well, He knows our desperate need for mercy.
- God's *grace* can be trusted because it is never revoked or withdrawn. He gladly gives His saving grace and lavishly pours out His sustaining grace.
- God's *love* can be trusted because nothing . . .

> nothing . . .
>> nothing . . .
>>> nothing . . .

separates us from His unconditional love.

A writer friend of mine, Bryan Jeffery Leech, defined this thought of trusting God in a more personal way when he wrote,

Father, during this coming week there may be times when I shall not be able to sense Your presence or to be aware of Your nearness.

When I am lonely and by myself
I trust you to be my companion.

When I am depressed and anxious
I trust you to lift my spirits.

When I am crushed by responsibility and overwhelmed by the demands of people on my time
I trust You to give me poise and a sense of purpose.

When I am rushed and running

I trust you to make me still inside.

When I forget You
I trust that You will never forget me.

When I forget others
I trust You to prompt me to think of them
and,
When You take something or someone from me
that I want to keep;
when You remove the props I lean on for
comfort in place of You;

when You refuse to respond to my questions
and to answer my too-selfish prayers,

I will trust You, even then.

Trusting God is nothing new, especially for the most seasoned of God's saints. But our trusting the whole character of God, when walking on strange and torn up streets, and trusting Him for His sustaining grace in our unworld crises can certainly stretch us into some new and even risky dimensions.

A friend, Sue Lenzkes, once asked me if the emotional and physical pain I was going through at that time was redefining my faith and bringing new definitions to old words like *faith*, *hope*, and *joy*. I wasn't too sure I understood what she meant, then. But, after the room called grace, my thinking changed. I realized that God is still God, and I am still me—even if I now qualified as an unworld person. And I was now able to write down some words which did indeed redefine my faith.

Because of my painful journey, I could picture God as our heavenly Father with a heart full of loving concern and tender compassion for us, His children. I could even sense the pleasure and pride He took in each of us, His children. I could also see God the Father's:

- Unconditional love to His children
- Unbiased judgments and justice for His children
- Undaunted effort in His plan for His children
- Unchangeable purpose to bring about good for His children
- Unfailing mercy to His children
- Unlimited forgiveness for His children
- Unfathomable grace for His children
- Unbroken chain of blessings for His children
- Unconstrained joy and pleasure *over* His children

How wonderful to understand that as we venture out—seeing God in new light, taking our first small steps in learning to walk the pathways called trusting—God knows where we are, what we do, where we go, and has (according to David's Psalm 139) our days planned out for us before we are born.

Like a loving father who dreams and plans ahead for his child's needs and desires, God takes delight and pleasure in us. And when we sin, make a mistake, experience failure and loss, or suffer great tragedies . . . God builds back the bridges of restoration so that we may softly cross the swollen rivers beneath us and not be swept away.

Yet, there's something else here . . . for what I have observed in the room called grace can be summed up by understanding that real healing comes not from one direction, but from two.

Yes, healing does come from God. But *just* as remarkable as seeing and feeling *God* at work in our lives is the way God heals our brokenness by using other *people*. He uses people here on earth to carry out His plans for our recovery. It is God and people, hand in hand, which bring us safely back from the razor's edge of terror in our unworld ordeal.

Actually, God and people, in tandem, is hardly a new concept. Repeatedly in the Bible we see God working through people and people reflecting God. So there's nothing new here . . . or is there?

In remembering, I have ascertained that when I was barely existing in the daily milieu of suffering, torn to shreds by my unbelievable unworld explosions and unable to pull the tiny fragmented pieces of my soul and mind together, for me to suddenly understand a great theological concept involving God's forgiveness, grace, or restoration . . . even to see or to feel the most illustrious, inspiring, or colossal aspects of God's character . . . did not, in the midst of each painful crisis, seem to be quite enough. I wish I could say it was.

"Wait a minute, here!" I can hear you cry. "This is heresy! Are you writing right out loud, here on paper, that God is not enough for our hurts, and not enough to solve our problems? What do you mean, He's not enough?"

Obviously I'm not even suggesting that God is inadequate or somehow unable or unwilling to be all that we would need our God to be. I *am* saying that the Bible seems to consistently point out that the divine plan of God for our sin and forgiveness involved Him. However, God's divine plan for our restoration and healing involves God working through His listening people.

In the beginning, we are told, after God had observed all He had created, even Adam, God made the observation that it was not good for man to live alone. What could God have possibly meant? Wasn't the incredible relationship between God and Adam enough?

Apparently that was not in God's great plan. Man, God decided, was not to live alone. Adam was to have one of his "own kind," so God invented Eve. . . .

God knew only too well, back at the first edges of time,

that Adam would need a human relationship with Eve. He'd need a companion, a helpmate, a partner ... yes, one of his "own kind." How positively incredible!

God knew, too, how strategic and important good and healthy relationships would be to us as we lived out our lives here on earth. Someone once said, "All we really have here on earth are our relationships." How true. God's wise and special plan took into account that a baby would need its mother, a child would need his or her parents, and that we adults would need each other. God designed us so He knew what we needed. We need human hugs. We need people to sing songs, to pray, and to laugh and dance. We need the flesh and blood presence of a loved one and, at unworld times, we need the loving physical touch and audible words of others in order to survive.

How positively divine and brilliant. God—who even today sees our despair, who feels our pain, perhaps even more acutely than we—divinely put Himself and His people together, knowing we'd need both God and mankind, in tandem. Think of it—God, the holy and divine, paired and teamed up with fragile people ... just like you and me.

I was to learn, that first fall and winter in Texas, just how beautifully this transaction of healing works between God and people.

It seems to me that God makes the first move. Knowing our brokenness, and on our behalf, He speaks to His other children who are *listening* to Him. After that, He moves their hearts with so much conviction and compassion that they act on what they heard in their hearts and carry out God's plan. They become heaven-sent ambassadors of loving care. Those caring people, whether they are a pastor, a member of the church, a neighbor, a co-worker ... no matter what their vocation demands of them ... as listening people of God, begin to do His will. They look around within the sphere of their own world. They fulfill their spiritual destiny and become committed to finding the wounded souls around them who need the touch of God's wholeness.

And let me tell you, these listening people of God, these real bona fide Christians *do find us!* They become, as it were, the everlasting arms of God around us during our unworld ordeals. They hold us, in the name of God, until our broken lives can be brought back together again. They become God's fingers which tenderly wipe the tears off our weeping hearts. They feed us God's homemade chicken soup to nourish us and strengthen our starving souls. They sing us God's very own songs of Zion . . . verse and chorus after chorus of hope . . . so that we feel enchanted, once more, with life's little joys. And not content to leave it at that, they—reflecting all the beauty of Christ around us—come to us. Not to preach, not to judge, or not to straighten out our lives . . . but, quietly and unobtrusively, just to sit on our front porch a spell. They sit, holding our hand, and just wait with us through the stillness of the dark night.

I don't know whether God *has* to have people do His work for Him or not. I don't know whether He *needs* people, or if He just designed it that way. (It seems to me, if I were in God's position, I'd just skip all the middlemen and zap the problem with a clean cut miracle . . . but then who's asking me?) So the why's and wherefore's of God's *methodology* are really not the issues here. It appears that when God wants to do something for a wounded person, He most often works through another person to carry it out.

When God wants to feed a hungry child, a family, or a nation . . . He has *people* do it.

When God wants to minister to those in prison . . . He has people do it.

When God wants to comfort those who mourn . . . He has people do it.

When God wants to preach the gospel to people all over the world . . . He has people do it.

When God wants to show us His face of kindness, mercy and grace . . . He has people do it.

When God wants to heal and restore our relationships with each other . . . He uses people to do it.

And when God wants us to hear the music once again . . . He uses people to do it.

If I thought the lessons I learned in the cabin about trusting God's marvelous character were revealing and restorative, I had a much bigger surprise awaiting me because God started the tandem procedures and began working in the very midst of my hell through His people.

People? Yes! Isn't that funny? Remember in my unworld holocaust it was people . . . good Christian people who were the very ones giving me the hardest time and pulverizing my soul with their stones. It was God's people who were the most verbal and who spared me nothing of their indignant wrath.

Very interesting . . . How could God use His children to comfort me, I wondered? How could they bind up my wounds? It seemed to me that it was people, good people, and my relationships with them that were all messed up. But, I guess God's plan took all that into account and He hand-picked His own listening people for the work of healing my shattered heart and mind.

I've already mentioned the first caring people who came to me, at the cabin. But, God sent others . . . not tons of people, mind you, just a few of the right ones. They were like the tiny sprinkles of a fine misty rain which comes sparkling through the morning sunshine, leaving everything bright and fresh with hope.

There were some rare authors who visited me at the cabin. Their unconditional support reminded me of the biblical story about Aaron and Hur and their gift of undaunted support to Moses. Exodus 17 recalls that during Israel's battles, their leader, Moses, would go to the top of the highest hill. There he would lift his hands heavenward and, as long as the soldiers could see him, Israel's army was victorious. But, if Moses grew tired and put his hands down, Israel would lose, and the enemy would win. During one such battle, Moses apparently grew tired and could no longer hold his arms up. So Aaron and Hur sat Moses down on a rock. Then, with Aaron on one side and Hur on the other, they stood there holding up the arms of Moses so his "hands were steady until the going down of the sun" and the victory was theirs!

Other authors nourished my ailing spirits with their kind words or their warm and encouraging letters.

Of my publishers, there were a few who affirmed me and some, at least in their silence, did not attack me.

There were two or three pastor friends who took the time to send warm handwritten notes of encouragement.

But the wonderful and surprising thing was that some letters came from pastors and missionaries I'd never met. Somehow they had heard of my separation and pending divorce, and their message, in essence, was their desire to assure me that God had given me special talents and gifts, and had called me to minister to hurting people. They were kind enough to suggest that God would use my present suffering to widen that very calling.

Twice I was given the privilege of speaking, in those months at the cabin. I spoke for a large conference of United Methodist Men in Texas, and for the annual conference of the Disciples of Christ denomination. I spoke haltingly, for the first time, about the "unworld" trauma. I'm not sure I did too much for them—but the people in these meetings poured out their love to me by writing very special, loving letters. The pastors from both these protestant denominations were most caring and the change was most healing to me. I was, and *am*, deeply grateful to them for being listening people of God.

There are two pastors who stand out the most in my mind. It was rather as though God propelled both of them to do a special work in my life and with the life of Francis. God seemed to give these pastors a divine imperative that somehow commissioned them to minister to us with all their wisdom and strength. They were undaunted in their loving efforts to bring God's healing love and restoration to our battered souls and grieving emotions.

One was the pastor in Mexia, Texas, who is named in the dedication of this book—Dr. Charles Rice. He is a United Methodist minister who phoned me when he learned from the Wiggins family that I was at the cabin, and pledged his ministerial support for me.

He became a true *servant* of God, one of those *listening* children of God. He was the one pastor who, after hearing my unworld facts and experiences, left his desk, knelt down beside my chair, and pointed out that it was time for me to "move on" to resurrection .... "Enough of crucifixion," he said, while the tears streamed down both our faces. I feel certain there will not be one but several stars in that dear servant of God's crown one day in heaven!

The other pastor who touched our hearts and lives, like our special Charles, was my father—Pastor Clifford Andrew Miller.

If you read *Irregular People*, you may have guessed that at least one of the irregular relationships in my life was the one I had with my father.

Through a strange set of circumstances, I got a call from my dad in 1984, during the height of marital conflict, and before our official separation.

The previous winter I had appeared on Gary Collins's national TV show, and some relatives had seen it in Michigan. Not too long after that show had aired, my dad went back home for his brother's funeral. While he was there his kinfolk told him, in no uncertain terms, that he was my irregular person.

Dad called me after he got back to California, on the suggestion of my sister, Marilyn. And, for the first time I could ever remember, he wanted to have a discussion as a father to his daughter about our relationship. Mostly, he wanted to know if he was my irregular person, and if that was true . . . did I hate him?

For years I had fantasized how that conversation would go, but never in the wildest scenarios of my mind did I dream it would actually take place or move us out of our fifty-year-old inability to communicate. It was one of those mysterious, long reaching ways of God working through His people to bring about the restoration of a relationship.

That night Dad and I talked honestly and openly, and for a long time, about the past hurts. Suddenly, I knew that after everything else was discussed, all *I* wanted to hear was, "Joyce, I love you," and all *he* wanted to hear was, "Daddy, I love you." So I proposed the idea that we put the past hurts to rest; he accepted that instantly, and we both wept as the fragrance of forgiveness engulfed us. Then, I repeated over and over again, "Daddy, I love you with all my heart."

Elizabeth, my precious stepmother, was on the extension, and I heard my dad fairly shout, "Did you hear that, Elizabeth? She doesn't hate me—*she loves me!*"

Although I was in my fifties, the conversation that night introduced me to the father I never knew I had. During that phone call I lost track of all the times *he* verbalized the never-before spoken words, "I love you, Joyce!"

After we said good night, and though it was very late, I went for a walk, by myself, to sort out all I'd heard my dad say. I wondered why, after all those years, God had suddenly moved in such a beautiful way, healing both our grievous wounds in one fell swoop . . . one phone call. What are the words? . . . "In God's time He makes all things so beautiful." . . . Hang on, dear hurting person . . . in His time . . . in His time. . . .

A few months later, when my separation occurred, I found I didn't have the courage to call Dad to tell him about it. I just couldn't bear to tell him such an unthinkable thing. He had been an old-fashioned fundamental preacher, a minister of God for over fifty years, and I had heard most of his sermons against divorce. I didn't want to risk spoiling our newly established relationship, just as it was beginning to blossom, by displeasing him. I needn't have worried.

Finally, one night, with fear and trembling, I called Dad. Hesitantly I told him I was separated and that I didn't see too much hope for a reconciliation. Nothing I'd known before prepared me for his *instant* response. It was a genuine spontaneous invitation to come live with him . . . so that he could take care of me! He ended our long conversation by emphatically saying, "Joyce, you are my darling daughter. I love you. And if you want to come live with Elizabeth and me, we'll take care of you and protect you!"

Recently Elizabeth told me that God had been preparing both of them for this eventuality . . . so my unworld tragedy did not surprise or shock them.

The incredibly satisfying relationship with Dad and Elizabeth did nothing but grow lovelier each and every day after that initial phone call.

Just before I left California to come to Texas, my dad called, and his voice was like a little kid's, enthusiastic and fairly jumping up and down with excitement. He said, "Joyce, I've got some *great* news for you . . . I almost called you late last night!" Then he shouted, "Are you ready? This is for you. It's my *best* gift . . . it's just for you!"

"Yes," I replied. (I needed *some* good news, and was very curious as to what in the world his "gift" would be.) "Tell me about it, Daddy."

Twice he read me these words:

> "Do not follow where the path may lead.
> Go instead, where there *is* no path.
> And leave a trail behind.

Over and over, for the next half hour, he told me that those words were my legacy, my inheritance, that he had nothing else materially to give me, but that he felt these words were just *meant* for me. I think now it was his way of giving me permission to make my own choices, no matter how difficult, and it was also his way of giving me his *unqualified* blessings. How right he was. Those words were his finest gift—ever—to me. That dear father of mine knew that a gift of words, poignant words . . . words that made sense and touched the very essence of my being . . . those words would mean the most to me.

Especially now. For from that first healing phone call (in the fall of 1984) to the day of his death (in June of this year, 1987), the bridge of love was solidly and beautifully constructed between us. He has left me with a storehouse full of rich memories to treasure and to hold me for the rest of my life.

How kind of God, to bring me full circle with my father, to give me these brief but glorious years with him—erasing and putting to rest the bad times of the past. I have no idea if God will choose to work exactly like this in any difficult and irregular relationship you might have. But, at least I'm aware, very aware, that while sometimes it seems totally impossible, healing can take place . . . even in the most long-standing and painful family relationships.

I am forever grateful to God that His plan for the restoration and wholeness for our lives, more often than not, means God working *through* His people.

Today I wrote this letter.

Dear Daddy,

Francis and I are sending our love to you. We thank you for the wonderful memory of singing with you in the nursing home just a few days before you left us. My, how we loved seeing you spring buoyantly back to life as you sang. We will never forget you or the sound of your voice.

After your funeral, Elizabeth gave us your old but treasured violin. Since you bought it several years before I was born, I can't remember a time without it or a home without its music. It rests in its case, by my piano, and each time I see it, my heart and mind hear the sweet way you made it sing.

Oh, yes, remember the gift of words you gave me a few years ago? Well, I took that gift to heart. I didn't go on the well-established path ... even the ones others declared I should follow. I'm making my own path, and it's sure scary at times, but I know God is leading me, and I am leaving a trail behind. I thank you for giving me your permission and approval of the path I did choose. But most of all, thank you for leaving me your blessings to walk where there *is* no path.

By now I'm sure you and Mother have had a glorious reunion ... give her a special hug and kiss for us. Wouldn't she have *adored* Francis? Also, be sure and tell all our loved ones up there in God's balcony that we hear them cheering us on ... and before too long, Daddy, we'll meet again.

Until then, your children call you blessed and I remain your darling daughter whom you loved and who dearly loves you.

Lovingly,

Joyce

During my autumn at the cabin, I joined the ranks of the

"newly divorced," as my mother would have put it ... but God continued to bind up my unworld wounds by His spirit and with His people.

The mail that continued to flow into Mexia came from thousands of people, most of whom I'd never personally met. It was an outpouring of God's love such as I have never seen (or felt) in all my years as a Christian woman.

The letters these people wrote were not mere form letters, or even thank you letters for some book, tape, or film which had touched their lives. These letters were of great beauty and all seemed to have one very consistent strain of thought and message. Continually, people assured me that while they knew (at least in part) of my "circumstances," they felt the details were none of their business, but rested between God and me.

The real message conveyed in their letters was that at some time in the past I had written or said something that ministered to them and now, because of my unworld agony, they wanted to minister to me. They felt now was *their* God-given opportunity to bear *my* burdens for me, to hold me up, and to pour the soothing oil of compassion on my raw and torn up life. Talk about God speaking to His listening people and then *their* response to the wounded!!

These were the people, who by their letters, became the loving body and face of God to me. Their words, reflecting God's face, blocked out the other painful people in my life and allowed me a fresh start, a brief rest for my weary soul, and a chance to catch my breath and move a little closer to some semblance of wholeness. Oh, did it feel good.

Even with the help of Ginger Williams, my secretary, I couldn't keep up with the enormous volume of mail; so, at one point, after some healing had taken place, I wrote this letter to as many as I could. In part, it read like this:

There is one word which describes the mail that reaches my little cabin in Texas and that is . . . *awesome.*

I smile, I weep, I heal, and I feel the very vigor of God strengthening and binding my broken spirit back together again as I read many letters I receive each day.

Did all of you attend a large secret convention recently, and did you all decide to write *exactly* the same letter, paragraph by paragraph? Did you all purpose in your hearts that because I ministered to you in your time of need that now, in my time of extreme loss and need, you would reach out to me and touch me with God's love? Since the mail comes from Africa, England, Australia, and all the states between Alaska and Florida, I must conclude that it was our loving heavenly Father who urged you to share your feelings and to pour out God's unconditional love on my open wounds.

Just a few days ago I went back to writing. I have no idea if anyone will publish my work, but I wanted you to know that as God gives me the insight to write, my first book will be dedicated to all of you; you who have not rubbed the salt of rejection nor dropped the stones of judgments into the raw gaping wounds of my heart. And because I've walked the path of suffering, both physical and emotional, for so long, I want to express my love and gratitude to those of you who have given so freely of God's unconditional love. The Christian world needs to know how you, in honest reality, carried out the verse, "Bear ye, one another's burdens."

Should God open the doors for my manuscript's publication, please know it was written for you, for clearly, I have seen the face of God in your letters and calls, and I will never be the same for the outpouring of your love!

This moment, I hug you.

Love,

Joyce Landorf

God Will Waste Nothing

*You must learn, you must let God teach you, that the
only way to get rid of your past is to get a future out
of it. God will waste nothing. There is something in
your past—something, if it be only the sin of which
you have repented—which, if you put it into the
Saviour's hands, will be a new life to you.*

—Dr. Phillips Brooks

9

The new year came to Mexia, Texas, and much to my surprise, I discovered I was alive! The winters of my unworld agony had not killed me! I had managed to survive—to wait, as Karen had said, for spring. And, I'll tell you . . . you who are mired in the snowdrifts of your unworld winter, spring's performance is definitely worth the wait.

My cabin on the lake was surrounded by the splendid symphony of spring. Oh, yes, I know it brought—as I've already mentioned—the first flood in several years, and the aftermath of roaches and snakes. But still, there was the healing going on slowly within me and I could hear the music of spring around me.

It was as though Arthur Fiedler personally directed the Boston Pops orchestra in a concert on my front lawn, and God set off a dazzling display of fireworks above the lake. Simply spectacular!

Along with trees covered with bright green leafy buds bursting on every limb, there was all kinds of new growth on the wisteia vines, promising the future arrival of pale lavender blossoms. There were Mrs. Lindley's daffodils lined up in rows, standing in front of her house like little ornamental yellow fences. Mr. Tacker had fixed and replaced all the broken flooring on the outside decks around the lake sides of the cabin so I could go sit out there. I watched the newest of baby birds, the magnificent blue herons, the wild ducks, and the Texas-sized panoramic sunsets of spring.

Somehow, I always have connected the word *spring* with the word *beginning* because spring brings closure to winter and blossoms with promises of new and fresh starts. Spring is not only a time of new life in all of nature but for people as well.

To me, moving from the wintry crucifixion of my un-world existence to the springtime of resurrection was quite definitely enhanced by David's 37th Psalm. That beautiful passage came into focus quite clearly during spring because it offered so much hope and promise of new beginnings.

I read and reread the passage from the King James Bible,

> Fret not thyself because of evil doers, neither be thou envious against the workers of iniquity. For they shall soon be cut down like the grass, and wither as the green herb.
>
> Trust in the Lord and do good; so shalt thou dwell in the land, and verily thou shalt be fed.
>
> Delight thyself also in the Lord; and he shall give thee the desires of thine heart.

I was clearly reminded that incredible spring that God, indeed, was helping me to not fret so much about the "evil-doers" of my life or be envious of anyone else.

The message here, directly to my heart, was for me to get on with my newfound ability to trust God, to do good, the best I possibly could, to dwell in the safety of the land, and thereby be fed and satisfied, and to delight myself in God.

It seemed those were the new beginnings of spring, and the words about God giving me the "desires of my heart" were to my unworld ordeal, the promises of spring.

Spring gave me, that year, several of my heart's desires. I recalled that high—possibly "first"—on my "desires" list was the desperate wish to be out of pain. Perhaps this "heart's desire" is at the top of your list as well. Oh how I pray you are encouraged by my story to hang on and that God grants you, as He has for me, some of your heart's desires.

Here is an excerpt from a letter I wrote that spring which was the chronology of my heart's desires come true:

I have found that putting back together the shattered pieces of one's life is a day and night full-time job which takes enormous energy. Even my children have questioned, "But, Mom, what do you actually do all day?" Yet, how can anyone explain the profoundly disturbing years of adjustment, the stress preceding and following a death, a divorce, a career change, or even a relocation? Or how can one estimate the damage these changepoints will cause on family, friends, and personal relationships? Worse yet, can we even "prepare" ourselves to handle and cope with life if these things happen? I doubt it.

Yet I find myself awestruck with the outpouring of God's love, mercy, and grace. He has granted what I can only describe as, three very healing miracles in my life.

The first miracle was physical in nature, and began on the day of my separation in 1984. The high levels of TMJ pain dropped dramatically. Since then, the pain has been extremely manageable and has gone from 25 to 30 days a month to less than 1 or 2 days a month. For all of the ten years of TMJ pain, the combination of the physical exhaustion and the emotional stress in my marriage, robbed me of any will to live. So, at this time, to be out of pain is an incredible answer to my deepest heart cries.

The second miracle was a healing of memories for me, and came as a wonderful surprise. For somehow, through all of the hurt and pain of my experiences, a warm and beautiful reconciliation blossomed between my father and myself. It was as if an impenetrable wall, which had separated us, crumbled and disappeared. The marvelous loving joy between us is genuine, positive, and very healing. Dad is in his eighties, and I am thrilled to be a part of sharing these years with him and his beloved Elizabeth.

The third miracle was purely personal. It was a miracle where the Lord did indeed give me my "heart's desire."

To those of you who did not suspect the trying circumstances of my past, and who had no knowledge of the deep agony of my problems, I know my divorce was very difficult for you to understand or accept. Many of you wrote of your sadness and shock, even grief upon hearing the news. But that divorce, as unthinkable and unbelievable as it was, *did* bring closure to the marriage last year.

Personally, it's been so long since I've "heard any music," both physically and emotionally, that I really began to wonder if forever I'd walk songless and alone in the valley of the wounded. I reached into the Psalms for my mother's favorite, Psalm 37. It tells of our committing, delighting, trusting, and resting, and then it speaks of God giving us the desires of our hearts. Over the years I have written out many "heart's desires" lists. But, not too long ago, I decided it was time to compose a new one. There were several "impossible dream" items, but at the top of the list was the wish and sincere heart's desire for God to put a very special love into my life. I never dreamed God would give me His finest gift in one extraordinary man—but He did.

We are so fortunate, as children of God, that our heavenly Father knows the desires of our hearts even better than we do.

You may be thinking that your heart's desires, as well as mine, are nothing but impossible dreams, unrealistic fantasies, and that spring will never rescue you from the winter of your despair. You need to know that I could not have fathomed, planned, or even suspected the turnings and the routing of my unworld journey—so I understand your reasoning. But try to hear me when I say (again), *God can be trusted and He works through people* for our unique healing.

With Karen Wiggins's hope-filled remark about my waiting for spring, the very week the peach trees bloomed in Central Texas Dr. Rice came to my cabin, performed the ceremony with Karen and Mark standing with us, and Francis and I were joined in marriage.

My list of "heart's desires" contains several other items that I shall not take the time to write out here—except for one.

That one heart's desire is about my personal mission statement and how it relates to you as hurting unworld people.

If Victor Frankl is correct, and I believe he certainly is on this issue, then we heal from our suffering and brokenness best when we can find meaning in it. If you were to ask me if there was any rhyme, reason, or meaning about these past years of my unworld travail, I'd shout *Yes!* Definitely yes, even though it's been excruciatingly painful and I came so close to giving up . . . still I now see some definite and positive patterns which have brought about or helped wholeness to take the place of brokenness.

I've learned that God's whole character can be trusted and that He *STILL* loves me. This is just as true for you, as it is for me!

In 1985, just before my offices were closed down, the author Tony Campolo phoned. He'd heard of my unworld circumstances and he wanted to make a brief comment. While I was too crushed, at the time, to assimilate the full impact of the message he left that day, nevertheless the truth of his words cannot be negated.

I write Tony's words here for you, dear hurting unworld person, because the same truths of his message for me apply to you.

> Convey to Joyce that we really love her. That what she's going through could enhance her ministry more in the long run as she gradually heals and then flows out again to people.
>
> Tell her, broken things actually make better vessels. God can use us *best* when we are totally broken.

So you see, no matter who you are, or whatever your unworld experiences . . . God can be trusted and He still loves you.

I've learned that my personal descent into my own unworld hell allowed me to earn some pretty unique credentials and qualified me to show the loving, caring face of God to people in the midst of their own unworld experiences.

I do believe there is a great deal of meaning to be found in our suffering . . . I'm also sure that, as the years go on, I will discover even more truths about unworld pain, about God, and about using these experiences for good.

Several years ago, before the major explosion of unworld factors took place in my life, I heard Millie Cooper tell of a true experience—about some handicapped children running a race. It profoundly touched me because I could see myself so clearly in the story. Today I see you, as well.

Millie told of attending the Special Olympics Games, and of an incident which happened during one of the races.

There were twenty-five or thirty handicapped, brain-damaged, or Down's syndrome kids lined up about to run this particular race around the track. Each runner had his or her own coach enthusiastically shouting last minute encouragement. The excitement was, as always in these events, cresting to a fevered pitch. Hundreds of people—parents, friends, and celebrities—were cheering and waving from the stands. No one missed the heady emotional significance of these kids, their race, or the moment.

Suddenly the starting gun went off and the race began. The youngsters ran down the dirt track all sort of clustered together, but it was a good beginning. However, not too many seconds after the race began, something went wrong. Apparently one of the runners near the center of the pack had fallen. The ones nearest to the boy who had fallen gave their full attention to picking him up. Other runners up ahead, who had gone on, now stopped, their faces registering confusion and consternation. They sensed something had gone badly for another runner, so, one by one, they went back to the child who had fallen.

All the runners seemed to make it their own individual responsibility to go back and see to the well-being of the child who was down. They were not satisfied to merely get the sobbing boy back up on his feet. They brushed his clothes, dried his tears, and tried, carefully, to remove the dirt and cinders off his knees, elbows, and forehead. *All* of the kids ministered to the one who had fallen . . . and, no, there is no better word than "ministered" because that's exactly what they did. Collectively, as with one heart and mind, they clearly stated that *nothing* was more important than tending to the needs of the one who was down.

Eventually the child was up on his feet, his tears were gone, and his cuts were determined to be minor; but still the other children grouped around him. Finally—by whatever means they used—the kids managed to get the boy laughing and in good spirits again about finishing the race. Then, as if by some special secret signal, they all turned and began to run. Together they ran . . . finishing the race with justifiable pride and honor.

I sat there and wept as I listened to Millie tell this story because I could envision myself as a fallen runner, and I could see that all around me were others . . . down, unable to run, and too broken to move—much less run.

"My God," I thought. "I am just like that special child who has fallen. I am flat on my face. The dirt and cinders have ground up my knees, elbows, and forehead into bloody shreds. It feels as though I've broken every bone in my body. The pain is blinding and almost as bad as the humiliating disgrace and embarrassment of the fall itself.

"I feel so alone, so left behind, and while I know other runners are down—still my own pain consumes me. I can tell that people I thought were running the race with me have run on ahead. Some have even called over their shoulder how stupid it was of me to trip over my own feet. Why is it no one stops? Doesn't anyone care? 'It's the race that's important!' someone calls from the sidelines. Is it? I wonder. What about me?"

All I could do was weep.

That was three years ago, and I now know that my picture of myself and others lying face down on the track was a real one. . . . But, just as I was about to believe I'd been abandoned and left there forever, God whispered to a few of His people who were listening. One by one at first, then a few at a time, those beautiful listening people heard the Lord, ascertained the seriousness of my pain, stopped their own race, came back, and began to minister to me.

Because of God and His people I am up on my feet again! They have brushed away the cinders and dirt. They have listened to my tears and dried my face. They have washed my wounds and soothed the cuts with heavenly ointment. They have set the broken bones of my emotions and put in gentle splints to aid healing.

They have given me a helping hand to get up, and they do not let go. They stand tall and hold me as I lean on them. They patiently walk with me while I try to limp forward. They entertain me by quietly humming a tune in my ear. They tell me a funny thing that happened to them in their race yesterday.

So because of God and His people I'm up and walking again. Mind you, I'm not running pell mell down this race track with the finish tape in sight, but I am up and walking. Actually it would be highly unrealistic of me to say I am up and vigorously running the race. It's too unrealistic for this early in my stages of recovery.

Walking in the valley of the wounded, as I said in the preface, is not soaring up with eagles' wings, or running without weariness . . . it is walking, just walking and not falling down or fainting. The running comes later with spring . . . and in God's own magnificent timing.

So you, down there on that unworld track, flat on your face, don't try to move. I know it's hard for you to hear this, because of the loud tumultuous sound of throbbing pain, but *help is on the way.*

There are lots of us listening people of God, who have heard of your unworld tragedy, and we care. We saw you back there behind us, when you fell. We've stopped our race, turned, and we're on our way back to you.

Try not to be afraid. Make the endeavor to hang on and wait for God's timing for spring. Soon we'll be there to help you up, bind up those ugly wounds, hold and carry you if we have to, until you're well enough to resume the race.

Since we are unworld people, we know your range of feelings and the emotional trauma you're going through. We know the humiliation, pain, rejection, and the dark despair which blinds you to any hope of running again. But we who have run and fallen before, know something else. We know about God's room called grace. Just wait until you get there! Right now waiting for help is painful, arduous, and at times quite lonely . . . but waiting does bring the wholeness and healing of spring. So try to wait.

Until spring comes for you, until winter's ice begins to thaw, we'll be the arms, the face, and the healing spirit of God for you. Just you wait. Soon you'll sense the newness of spring's beginnings.

Your pain will ease. Your wounds will heal. Your broken bones will knit together, and you'll be ready to run, with head and heart held high, the race that's set before you.

We'll run together, you and I. We'll keep a listening ear open to the whisperings of God. We'll also keep a watchful eye out for others behind us who trip and fall on the unworld track. We'll keep a caring heart ready to bind up others' wounds in the name of God.

But in the meantime, dear unworld person, while you wait for spring, this is my heartfelt prayer for you,

> May the Lord bless and protect you; may the Lord's *face radiate with joy because of you;* may he be gracious to you, show you his favor, and give you his peace.

Numbers 6:24–26
The Living Bible